The Photographs Of David Octavius Hill And Robert Adamson

Keith Bell
Curator

David Harris
Associate Curator

Essays By
Keith Bell
David Harris
Grant Arnold

Mendel Art Gallery
Saskatoon Canada

Published for the exhibition
*The Photographs of David
Octavius Hill and Robert
Adamson* by the Mendel Art
Gallery, a nonprofit
organization supported by
donations and grants from the
City of Saskatoon, Province of
Saskatchewan, Saskatchewan
Arts Board, The Canada
Council, and Museum
Assistance Programmes of the
National Museums of Canada.

Photography:Cats. 120,126 by
BP Photo Services, Saskatoon.
All works from the collection
of the Scottish National
Portrait Gallery by Tom Scott,
Edinburgh. All other
photographs courtesy of the
Glasgow University Library,
Glasgow.

Designer: McKay Goettler &
Associates, Saskatoon

Printer: Houghton Boston,
Saskatoon

Typesetting: The Type Source,
Saskatoon

Mendel Art Gallery
950 Spadina Crescent East
P.O. Box 569
Saskatoon, Saskatchewan
Canada S7K 3L6
(306) 975-7610

COVER
Cat. 3 *Rev. Thomas Blizzard Bell*

CONTENTS

Lenders To The Exhibition

Glasgow University Library
Glasgow, Scotland

Scottish National Portrait Gallery
Edinburgh, Scotland

Itinerary

Mendel Art Gallery
Saskatoon, Saskatchewan
15 May to 21 June 1987

The Edmonton Art Gallery
Edmonton, Alberta
29 August to 15 October 1987

Art Gallery of Greater Victoria
Victoria, British Columbia
5 November to 20 December 1987

Art Gallery of Ontario
Toronto, Ontario
23 March to 8 May 1988

Cat. 76 *Mrs. Cleghorn and John Henning as Miss Wardour and Edie Ochiltree from Sir Walter Scott's "The Antiquary"*

FOREWORD

LINDA MILROD
DIRECTOR

David Octavius Hill and Robert Adamson began their professional collaboration in 1843. The partnership lasted less than five years, but the breadth, the quality and the sheer volume of their production had a lasting effect on succeeding generations of photographers.

This exhibition, *The Photographs of David Octavius Hill and Robert Adamson*, celebrates the results of their collaboration, and the essays which follow examine three central issues. In his article, Keith Bell, assistant professor, Department of Art and Art History, University of Saskatchewan, and curator of the exhibition, discusses the social and political attitudes which influenced Hill and Adamson's Newhaven work. David Harris, assistant to the curator of photography, the Canadian Centre for Architecture, Montreal, and associate curator of the exhibition, has concentrated his research on the photographic portraiture of Hill and Adamson, relating it to the painterly tradition from which it emanated. Grant Arnold, extension coordinator, the Mendel Art Gallery, has provided us with a succinct history and description of the calotype process favored by the partners.

The works in *The Photographs of David Octavius Hill and Robert Adamson* were borrowed from two major public collections in Scotland. The Glasgow University Library in Glasgow maintains a valuable collection of vintage prints, as well as original negatives, which has, until now, been little known. Edinburgh's Scottish National Portrait Gallery, the other lender to the exhibition, holds the largest collection of photographs by Hill and Adamson in the world. The Mendel Art Gallery is proud to bring both the work of Hill and Adamson and the wealth of these collections to international attention. It is also fitting that this exhibition open in Saskatoon where both the Mendel Art Gallery and The Photographers Gallery — the latter one of Canada's oldest existing institutions dedicated to knowledge of photography — have presented exhibitions of historic and contemporary photographs to appreciative and supportive audiences.

The Mendel Art Gallery is grateful to many who have facilitated this important exhibition. The Glasgow University Library and the Scottish National Portrait Gallery, through their curatorial representatives, Nigel Thorp and Sara Stevenson respectively, have not only generously agreed to lend large numbers of works, but have been extremely helpful both throughout the period of the exhibition research, and with the complicated practical demands that characterize international arrangements. We are grateful to them both and are very pleased that each has contributed to this publication.

Seven photographs in *The Photographs of David Octavius Hill and Robert Adamson* are modern salted paper prints. They were made from the original negatives specifically for this exhibition by Michael Gray of Monmouth Calotype, Bath, England. We are grateful to him for providing us with photographs that so closely approximate vintage material.

Keith Bell brought the idea for the exhibition to the Mendel Art Gallery in the fall of 1984. We thank him for developing the concept, for guiding the progress of the exhibition, and for carrying out the project with enthusiasm and expertise. We are also very grateful to David Harris. His assistance with the exhibition research and the contribution of his fine text have significantly enhanced the quality of this exhibition.

The staff of the Mendel Art Gallery is to be congratulated for successfully organizing the exhibition, and two deserve special mention here. Grant Arnold not only contributed to the exhibition catalogue but acted as institutional liaison for all phases of the exhibition's development. Sylvia Tritthardt, registrar, supervised the care and handling of these extremely fragile works. We thank these individuals as well as all the Gallery staff for ensuring the success of the exhibition.

This exhibition has been funded in large part by the Museum Assistance Programmes of the National Museums of Canada. We are grateful for their contribution to the exhibition research, production of the exhibition catalogue, and the national touring costs.

We also sincerely appreciate the generous support of The British Council. This international agency recognized the value of presenting the work of significant Scottish artists to Canadian audiences and provided valuable financial assistance towards the research and production of *The Photographs of David Octavius Hill and Robert Adamson*.

GLASGOW UNIVERSITY LIBRARY

NIGEL THORP

Visitors to Glasgow are often surprised to find that an ancient University should possess, alongside its priceless manuscript and rare book collections, a unique resource for the study of early photography. Considering the difficulty and the cost of making a historical collection today, when photography has become established as a subject for the student as much as for the amateur, the University Library is fortunate in having acquired many items of photographic interest when they were first produced during the nineteenth century. The most important groups of early photographic material were, however, acquired from an enthusiastic twentieth-century collector, Robert O. Dougan, who devoted his efforts over many years to rescuing what earlier generations had overlooked.

The most remarkable feat of Mr. Dougan's collecting activity was to acquire literally hundreds of calotype negatives and prints made in the mid-1840s by the most illustrious of the early Scottish photographers, David Octavius Hill and Robert Adamson. Hill and Adamson's pioneering work was conducted for the most part from a studio in Rock House on Calton Hill in Edinburgh. When Adamson's early death in 1848 brought this partnership to an end, Hill, the artist, could find no satisfactory substitute for the skills of his chemist friend and largely abandoned his active interest in photography. While many examples of their work had been distributed or sold, large numbers of negatives and prints remained in the Calton Hill studio for the next hundred years, being handed down from one occupant to the next, until they were sold to Robert Dougan in 1943. When Mr. Dougan left his job as city librarian in Perth to pursue his career abroad, first in Ireland and subsequently in the United States, he offered the major part of his collection, including the Hill and Adamson works, to the Glasgow University Library, convinced that a permanent home should be given in Scotland to such an important national collection.

This Hill and Adamson material has been known, hitherto, only to a small number of photographic historians. It is very pleasing now to see that it can be appreciated by a much wider international audience, and we are glad to welcome the initiative of the Mendel Art Gallery which has made this possible.

Scottish National Portrait Gallery And The Scottish Photography Archive

Sara Stevenson

The world's largest collection of the calotypes taken by David Octavius Hill and Robert Adamson is contained in the Scottish National Portrait Gallery in Queen Street, Edinburgh. The Gallery owns some five thousand items, negatives and positives, which include twenty-three hundred different images. The photographs came to the Gallery from four main sources. In 1928, James Brownlee Hunter bequeathed a collection of two thousand calotypes which he had purchased in an auction room, some of which had originally belonged to the painter, James Drummond (a friend of Hill). This gift was followed by the purchase in 1937 of four albums from the Finlay estate, after the death of Sophia Finlay more than ninety years after she had been photographed by Hill and Adamson (cat. 74). In 1950, the Gallery was given five hundred negatives and seven hundred prints from the collection of the bookseller, Andrew Elliot, himself a great enthusiast for Hill and Adamson's work who had planned the first published book on their photographs.[1] Twenty-nine further photographs were bought in 1975 when the Royal Scottish Academy sold D.O. Hill's own albums.[2]

In the last two years the Gallery has been actively adding to its photography collection. Our new remit allows us to collect fine photographs by Scots, or by non-Scots taken in Scotland, regardless of subject matter. We have also set up the Scottish Photography Archive to collect information on the Scottish photographers and to look at other collections with the aim of discovering where the important photographs are. The Gallery's collection has grown most impressively and many excellent new photographers have emerged from the search.

We are anxious to pursue the Scottish photographers working abroad and, in view of the numerous Scots who emigrated to Canada, feel confident that Canada will be a good hunting ground. William Notman and Alexander Henderson are notable as two of Canada's best photographers who were born in Scotland. We would be very grateful for any information on Scots-Canadian photographers and will be happy to offer any information we may have in return.

Such cooperation, as is evident in this exhibition, *The Photographs of David Octavius Hill and Robert Adamson*, provides an important opportunity for further study of this important art form.

1. Published by his son ANDREW ELLIOT [and others], comp., *Calotypes of D.O. Hill and R. Adamson Illustrating an Early Stage in the Development of Photography: Selections from His Collection by Andrew Elliot*, introductory essay, 'The Early History of Photography', by John M[iller] Gray, printed in a limited edition of thirty-eight copies for private circulation, Edinburgh (1928).

2. The fully illustrated catalogue of the Gallery's collection is still available. *David Octavius Hill and Robert Adamson: Catalogue of their calotypes taken between 1843 and 1847 in the collection of the Scottish National Portrait Gallery* (Edinburgh: Trustees of the National Galleries of Scotland, 1981).

INTRODUCTION

KEITH BELL

The collaboration of David Octavius Hill (1802-1870) and Robert Adamson (1821-1848) began with the origins of modern photography — a moment in history when the process seemed almost like alchemy and the pictorial possibilities excited a whole generation of artists. It is this moment in the history of European art that is celebrated in this exhibition — the first major retrospective in North America of the images of Hill and Adamson.

Photography as a practical method of representation dates from 1839 with the invention of the daguerreotype and calotype. It was just four years later in Edinburgh, Scotland, that the partnership of Hill and Adamson began. Their initial collaboration was prompted when a large number of ministers broke from the Church of Scotland to form a Free Church. Hill, a painter and illustrator, wanted portrait studies for his projected painting of the Disruption of the Church of Scotland, and it was suggested he work with Robert Adamson, who in 1843 had established a photographic business in Edinburgh. In the following five years, the partners not only recorded likenesses of the dissenting ministers but created a legacy of more than three thousand images, among them portraits of Edinburgh society, and photographs of Edinburgh and the surrounding countryside: the fishing village of Newhaven and its inhabitants, St. Andrews, the chapel at Roslin, Linlithgow, Ballochmyle and to the south, Durham Cathedral. Although the partnership lasted only five years — until Adamson's early death in 1848 — the approximately three thousand images represent prodigious numbers when one realizes that calotypes were generally taken out of doors and their production was largely curtailed during the winter months.

Hill and Adamson were among the first photographers to work consciously in a fine art context. They successfully took elements from an existing pictorial tradition and combined them with the intrinsic properties of the calotype process. In this exhibition, we have chosen to concentrate on the portraits and views of Edinburgh and Newhaven as being representative of the broad parameters of their artistic production. It is hoped that the sharing of these photographs with an international audience will increase knowledge on this continent of the definitive work of the partners and the process they utilized — the calotype.

The origins of modern photography lie within the development of the calotype in the mid-nineteenth century. The calotype allowed, for the first time, the creation of a number of positive prints from a single paper negative. This factor of reproductiveness gave the calotype a marked advantage over its rival, the daguerreotype, which produced only a unique image from which no additional copies could be made. Unlike the daguerreotype, which gave a consistently sharp and detailed image, that of the calotype was more diffused, depending, for its effect, upon strong painterly contrasts of light and shade. The calotype process is described in detail in the third of the following essays.

The photographic activities of Hill and Adamson have been documented and described extensively, and the essays in this catalogue are intended to complement the existing literature, as well as to highlight selected references within the exhibition. The first essay looks at Hill and Adamson's calotypes of the fisherfolk of Newhaven, and considers them in terms of contemporary middle-class attitudes to the working people of Scotland. The second essay discusses the portrait calotypes, their relationship to portrait painting, and the reactions of contemporaries to the images.

The partnership of David Octavius Hill and Robert Adamson lasted only a few years but the historical importance of their work and its consistently high quality have ensured the continuance of their reputation. In this exhibition and its accompanying catalogue, we have endeavored to give a clear picture of the richness and variety of their artistic production.

Cat. 103 *Mrs. Hall*

An Incalculable Number Of Fine Living Pictures: Hill And Adamson's Newhaven Calotypes

Keith Bell

During the last few years a considerable body of art historical literature, by John Barrell and others, dealing with the image of working people in nineteenth century art has emerged.[1] Such studies have provided extensive information not only about contemporary social and political conditions but also about the ways in which art was viewed during the period. Photographic historians, however, have not always been so quick to appreciate the possibilities of these studies, largely, perhaps, because some critics have always felt that photography, with its apparently "real" subjects and strong technological emphasis, has always *been* considered in social terms, for example, in studies of the development of travel photography or the *carte-de-visite*.[2]

This assumption is by no means accurate, however, and a tendency has developed which views certain photographic subjects — notably working-class ones — as so-called "documents" of past trades or industries about which we might feel either suitably nostalgic at their passing, or disturbed by the subjects' conditions of labor. In such cases, the approach is retrospective and does little to further our understanding of the meanings associated with images of working-class life during the period.

These approaches have clearly affected the way in which the work of David Octavius Hill and Robert Adamson has been studied in the past. For example, while the calotypes of their middle-class subjects have been discussed in some detail, the Newhaven views have received less attention from historians. One notable commentator, Roy Strong,[3] dismissed the images in a paragraph in which he described them as picturesque genre scenes which were mainly intended to show off the fisherwomen's remarkable costumes, and concluded by repeating (without comment) the well-known description of their appearance taken from *Chamber's Edinburgh Journal* of the 1830s and subsequently reprinted in 1838 in *A Series of Original Portraits and Caricature Etchings by the Late John Kay*.[4] At no time have the critics considered the Newhaven fisherfolk as an important part of a more extensive discourse on the condition of the working classes in Scotland during the first half of the nineteenth century, a discourse carried out, in the case of Newhaven, almost entirely by middle-class commentators who imposed their own values and concerns upon the community.[5] As members of that class, Hill and Adamson not only shared its attitudes, but also depended upon it as a market for their artistic production. This essay is intended to give a clearer idea of some of the complicated cultural and ideological attitudes which the photographers and their middle-class audience brought to the issues surrounding the Newhaven fisherfolk in the 1840s.

Cat. 110 *Mrs. Flucker*

The village of Newhaven is situated about three miles from the center of Edinburgh on the Firth of Forth. The port was founded in the fifteenth century for the purposes of ropemaking and shipbuilding. Subsequently, after the decline of these industries, Newhaven's prosperity was derived from the extensive oyster beds in the Forth and the seasonal herring fishery.[6] The produce of these two activities, together with a variety of white fish brought into the harbor by deep-sea fishing boats from other ports along the Scottish coast, was sold in the city of Edinburgh by the fishwives of Newhaven. These women — whose trade provided the principal family income — carried their produce into the city in wicker baskets or "creels," which were slung on their backs by means of a canvas strap passed across the forehead (cat. 104). They toured the residential neighborhoods (cat. 110) or sold their fish at the roadside, activities which were known collectively as "creel hawking."

By 1844-45, when Hill and Adamson took their photographs, this long-standing economic order had begun to change. The Scottish railway network had expanded to include most of the fishing ports, including Newhaven, and the deep-sea fishing boats could now bypass the port and send their produce directly to market.[7] As a result, the fishwives were forced to compete with the better capitalized fishmongers and barrow hawkers at central fish auctions, and their near monopoly on the Edinburgh market was broken. Subsequently, successful efforts were made to re-equip the Newhaven fishing fleet for the deep-sea fisheries, and the fishwives continued to creel hawk. Despite these improvements, however, the women were unable to regain their preeminence in the trade.[8]

Hill and Adamson first referred to the village in advertising their planned series of six volumes of calotypes, one of which was to be called *The Fishermen and Women of the Firth of Forth*, which they announced in the *Edinburgh Evening Courant* for 3 August 1844. Later, in April 1845, Hill informed the painter, David Roberts, that "we are preparing Fishwives for a book, and have done some fine things lately."[9] While this particular book was never produced, the Newhaven calotypes were included in a number of albums, subsequently put together by Hill and Adamson, which contained a broad cross section of the studio's production.

The potential reasons for Hill and Adamson's evident interest in the people of Newhaven, to the exclusion of other sections of the Scottish working classes, were numerous.

One of these was historical. Newhaven had a long and loyal association with the state, reaching back to the reign of James IV of Scotland, who had built the *Great Michael*, the largest ship in the Scottish navy, at the shipyard in Newhaven in 1507-11. While the

14

yard declined with James's death, the men from the fishing fleet, which rapidly grew up there, soon acquired a consistent reputation for loyalty. For example, in 1796 the Newhaven Society of Fishermen volunteered their services as a marine force to protect the coast against raids by the French. This act of loyalty, which was also a clever way of avoiding conscription and protecting their fishing interests, proved popular with both the Admiralty and the public, and the men were organized into a corps of Sea Fencibles with their own colors presented by the Lord Provost and Magistrates of the City of Edinburgh. This patriotic act was repeated in 1803, when the fishermen provided a crew of 200 for *H.M.S. Texel*, a ship-of-the-line, which quickly captured a French frigate, bringing the Newhaven crew a letter from George IV and a sum of £250 from the city treasury.[10]

Together with a sturdy reputation for patriotism, the Newhaven fisherfolk were also singled out as unusual or even exotic by the commentators who wrote about them in the nineteenth century. In part, this stemmed from their habit of marrying within the community and keeping themselves apart from the other trades — even within the Newhaven area. This aspect was remarked upon by James Colston in his book *The Town and Port of Leith: its Historical Connection with the City of Edinburgh* (1892), who reported that:

> The fishermen of Newhaven rarely intermarry even with the women of other fishing communities. A woman must be well acquainted with the preparation of nets and lines and the use of the oar, if she would become a thorough fisherman's wife. She must be able to don the creel and attend markets, or make her usual rounds of calling for the purpose of disposing of the fishes her husband has caught . . . .[11]

This insular life was made more interesting by various suggestions that Newhaven folk were descended from foreign stock, most probably from the Netherlands. For example, Mrs. Cupples, the first historian of the village, wrote in *Newhaven, its origin and history* (1888) that a Flemish colony "gave the place its earliest vigour in regard to industrial success."[12] She went on:

> To anyone who is personally acquainted with their village ways, their customs, idioms, family names, and costumes, it is often noticeable how much they resemble Flemish or Dutch fisherfolk . . . In complexion and general physique both sexes often exemplify an old Flemish descent; some being blonde, as any typical Netherlander; some dark as any typical Spaniard; comparatively few intermediate.

This was further enhanced by the women's extraordinary costume:

> . . . their manifold petticoats, striped in contrasted colours; peculiar short gowns, displayed bare arms with white elbow bands; bright head shawls; or in the case of the elder women, peculiar white linen caps; trim stockings . . . and neat serviceable shoes.[13]

Other writers suggested that the Newhaven fisherfolk were descended from French shipwrights who had remained in Scotland after working on the *Great Michael* in the sixteenth century. There was probably an element of truth in both suggestions, particularly the Flemish connection, although, if Mrs. Cupples had looked at fishing communities elsewhere in Scotland and England, she would have found similar insular customs, a distinctive sturdy appearance and equally exotic costumes.

Apart from their historic loyalty to the crown and reassuringly traditional appearance, the Newhaven fisherfolk also won the approval of Victorian commentators for their evident financial independence and ability to maintain their own poor. This particularly impressed Hugh Paton in 1838, when he remarked that the Society of Newhaven Fishermen acted as a benefit organization to oversee the poor and destitute; as he put it:

> A noble feature of the character of the Newhaven fishermen is their sturdy independence of spirit, and the respect they enforce due to old age. They maintain their own poor.[14]

This was particularly laudable at a time when the general condition of the working class in Scotland, impoverished by a series of depressions since the Napoleonic wars, had given the authorities serious cause for alarm. This state was highlighted by the collapse of the handloom industry in Paisley between 1841 and 1843; and the 1842 *Report on the Sanitary Condition of the Labouring Population of Scotland,* which investigated the spread of poverty in the once genteel neighborhoods of Edinburgh (High Street) and Glasgow.[15] In the 1840s, while Hill and Adamson were at work, the situation became so serious that some writers, like Lord Cockburn[16] (cat. 70), feared that the industrial working class, led by the Chartists, was on the edge of revolution.[17] In these circumstances, the Newhaven people were not only a suitably historic and picturesque subject for the Hill-Adamson camera, but were also exemplary and reassuring illustrations of industry and community, at a time when the Scottish middle classes were particularly sensitive about the image of working people and their potential for social unrest.

The approval with which most commentators greeted the Newhaven fisherfolk's financial independence and adherence to a traditional way of life also found its expression in frequent accounts of their dress and general appearance throughout the nineteenth century. These help to explain not only Hill's choice of the Newhaven women as his subjects, but also why he took such care to pose them with their costume displayed to its best advantage. One important example, first published in *Chamber's Edinburgh Journal* and extensively quoted by Hugh Paton in his commentary to the two-volume edition of *A Series of Original Portraits and Caricature Etchings by the Late John Kay* of 1838, established the norm for this approach:

A cap of cotton or linen, surmounted by a napkin tied below the chin, composes the investiture of the head; the more showey structures wherewith other females are adorned being inadmissable from the broad belt which supports the ''creel'', that is, fish basket, crossing the forehead. A sort of woolen pea-jacket, of vast amplitude of skirt, conceals the upper part of the person, relieved at the throat by a liberal display of handkerchief. The underpart of the figure is invested with a voluminous quantity of petticoat, of substantial material and gaudy colour, generally yellow with stripes, so made as to admit of a very free inspection of the article, and woven in such immense numbers, that the bare mention of them would be enough to make a fine lady faint. One half of these ample garments is gathered up over the haunches, puffing out the figure in an unusual and uncouth manner. White worsted stockings and stout shoes complete the picture. Imagine these investments indeed upon a masculine but handsome form, notwithstanding the slight stoop forward, which is almost uniformly contracted — fancy the firm but elastic step, the toes slightly inclined inwards — and the ruddy complexion resulting from hard exercise, perhaps sometimes from dram-drinking — and you have the *beau ideal* of fishwives (fig. 1).[18]

There were a number of reasons for this interest in traditional working-class costume: one, in particular, related to the changing social patterns of nineteenth century Britain, brought about largely by the industrialization of large parts of the countryside and the rapid growth of the cities. This led, or was believed to have led, to the abandonment of distinctive regional costume, and worse, as this often implied, the once clean divisions between different trades or classes. Indeed, the growing rigidity with which class distinctions were applied in Victorian Britain was symptomatic of the fears, held particularly by the middle levels of society, that the upward mobility of the new amorphous mass of the industrial working classes threatened not only their financial position, but also their distinctive outward appearance and, hence, their class identity.[19]

This attitude is at once apparent in a review on ''The Art of Dress'' written by Lady Eastlake and published anonymously in *The Quarterly Review* of December 1846, at a time when Hill and Adamson were probably busy photographing the Newhaven people.[20] While Lady Eastlake was unusual in that she maintained an active independent literary career — even after her marriage to Sir Charles Eastlake — her social attitudes were entirely typical of a woman of her class in Britain during the 1840s. Her lengthy review of three new books on fashion and costume was mainly taken up with a discussion of contemporary and historical dress. However, in the middle of a consideration of fifteenth century women's clothing, she suddenly digressed into a debate about the appropriateness of certain types of dress for different classes and races. Put a ''grand Italian Contadina'' in the dress of an English abigail (or serving maid) she suggests, and

an artist may discover some latent beauty, but the majority would condemn her as heavy, dingy, and decidedly plain . . . .

Fig. 1 *Edinburgh Fishwife.* From *A Series of Original Portraits and Caricature Etchings by the Late John Kay*

> Or look nearer home [she suggested] at the Newhaven woman, who seen every lawful day in her cap of Norman extraction, with a bright coarse handkerchief thrown carelessly at the back of it, exhibits always a fine strongly marked countenance, and often a very handsome one: and see the same woman on Sunday in a silk or velvet hat, with all due appurtenance of blonde lappets and artificial flowers, and you no longer recognize the common unmeaning face, which has lost all its real character in the attempt to assume one utterly foreign to it.[21]

Scarcely concealed in this statement is the assumption that any attempt by what Lady Eastlake called "our lower class of women" to step beyond the perceived boundaries of their social position can only result in the "handsome" countenance being instantly transformed into a "common unmeaning face, which has lost all its real character." Here, it seems to me, the author was determined not only to maintain a permanent division between the classes, but also to base that division on a form of hereditary inevitability, which assumed that anybody who attempted to cross that barrier would at once be revealed as an impostor.

For Lady Eastlake, and probably for her friend D.O. Hill, the continued adherence of the Newhaven people, at least on working days, to a traditional form of dress was not only quaint, but was also reassuring from the point of view of the proper social ordering of the classes, this last being tempered by her warning about the women's transgression of that order on Sundays when they donned the classless products of the new, mass-produced fashion industry. While Hill photographed nearly all the activities of the Newhaven fisherfolk (within the bounds of technical possibility), he notably omitted scenes of the women dressed in what they must have felt to be their Sunday best, preferring to confine his studies to their distinctive working attire. In taking these photographs, Hill also probably felt a real concern for the survival of the traditional Newhaven costume and way of life, and assumed a responsibility to record it.

A similar sense of history and dismay at the imminent passing of a traditional way of life had long been an established element of Scottish art and literature, notably in David Wilkie's popular painting, *Pitlessie Fair* 1804 (fig. 2) which, as well as recording a contemporary event, was probably also intended as a memorial to a traditional village fair. Similarly, as Lindsay Errington has pointed out, when Wilkie returned to Scotland in 1817 to collect accurate details for his painting of the *Penny Wedding*, he reported to a friend that in some ways the country reminded him of a living museum:

> Scotland is most remarkable . . . as a volume of history. It is the land of tradition and of poetry. Every district has some scene in it of real and fictitious events treasured with a sort of religious care in the minds of the inhabitants.[22]

Fig. 2 SIR DAVID WILKIE
Pitlessie Fair
1804
oil on canvas
58.5 × 106.7 cm
Collection: National Galleries of Scotland

Hill's own art continued in this tradition with his illustrations for Scott's novels in the 1830s, for the *Tales and Sketches of the Ettrick Shepherd* published by Blackie, and for the landscape plates for *The Land of Burns* in 1840. These were followed in 1847 by the well-received oil painting, *Edinburgh Old and New* (coll. National Galleries of Scotland), which followed Wilkie's *Pitlessie Fair* in representing the character of both the town and its inhabitants, although on a more allegorical level. Among the characters represented in Hill's painting was a group of fisherwomen, drawn from one of the Newhaven calotypes (cat. 104) and probably representing part of "Old Edinburgh." In England, Sir Charles Eastlake developed a more artificial variant of the theme with a series of highly fashionable society portraits, like that of Mrs. Charles H. Bellenden Ker dressed as an Italian contadina (or peasant), which Mrs. Bellenden Ker later bequeathed to Lady Eastlake (coll. London, Tate Gallery). Lady Eastlake also admired the sentimental rural subjects of her friend Edward Landseer, and the Scottish scenes of David Wilkie. When Wilkie's *Distraining for Rent* was exhibited at the Royal Scottish Academy in 1846, she recorded in her diary that,

Cat. 104 *Fishergirls*

> Wilkie's Distraining for Rent is matchless, every figure appropriate, natural and telling: not an over-acted expression — mere quiet sorrow and quiet indignation.[23]

In this description, Lady Eastlake found her working people, as she said, "appropriate" (a favorite word), "natural and telling." None of of them overreacts to their situation — that is, goes beyond the bounds of propriety; they are, in fact, operating within the constraints which she has laid down: that peasants should indeed appear, as they do in Hill and Adamson's calotypes, as so many "fine living pictures."[24]

Lady Eastlake's attitude was, of course, not in the least unusual among the middle- and upper-class consumers of art in the nineteenth century. As John Barrell demonstrated in *The dark side of the landscape: the rural poor in English painting 1730-1840*, the painting of rural subjects was a difficult profession, in which artists had to be careful to avoid anything which might spoil the tranquility of the landscape and the docility of their human subjects.[25] Country people were required to be hard working, happy and well fed, as they appeared in Gainsborough's landscapes and his depictions of peasant children. These latter almost suggest prototypes for Hill's Newhaven subjects, where the boys are shown by the boats (their future occupation — "his faither's breeks"), with the older girls minding the small children, that is, symbolic of their supposedly never changing cycle of life. By contrast,when the subjects appear idle, shifty, and therefore potentially subversive to the middle-class ideal, as in George Moreland's *The Alehouse Door,* the picture was condemned as being, according to Moreland's biographer writing in 1806,

> too low a subject to merit the same attention as several other pictures by the artist, who gave himself a latitude upon some occasions, that was very disgusting to an eye of taste.[26]

Closer to home, Wilkie's *Distraining for Rent* had provoked an even sharper call for artistic censorship when it was first exhibited in 1815, in the middle of the severe agricultural crisis following the end of the Napoleonic wars. One reviewer felt that the picture was "too sadly real," while another found it dangerously "liable to political interpretation," an opinion which contrasted to Lady Eastlake's view in 1846 after the social and political conditions had stabilized.[27]

Unlike Wilkie, Hill carefully avoided any social or political comment which might disturb the sensibilities of people like Lady Eastlake, who constituted the potential market for the planned Newhaven album. Hill's Newhaven is dilapidated but picturesque, and there is no sign of the piles of filth and rubbish which contemporary philanthropists identified as an undesirable and unhealthy feature of Scottish fishing villages. [28] In the same spirit, Hill's Newhaven fisherfolk are never portrayed as rough working people who were often dirty and exhausted in the pursuit of their trade. Instead, they frequently appear just as elegant as Zuccarelli's or Sir Charles Eastlake's peasant women, and just as unthreatening: that is, they conform very closely to Lady's Eastlake's requirements that peasants should be as pretty as so many "fine living pictures."

Another recurrent emphasis which preoccupied the predominantly male, middle-class commentators on Newhaven, beginning in the late eighteenth century, was the physical attractiveness of the fisherwomen. The idea that women belonging to the lower classes were in some way freer and more available was, in part, related to the origins of those women and girls who were forced to take up full- or part-time prostitution in the cities.[29] In the case of the fisherwomen, their independent business and daily absences from home led to implied doubts about their respectability, and also to a campaign (not unconnected with the commercial interests of the Edinburgh fishmongers) to persuade them to stay at home and care for their families.[30]

However, the admiration expressed by men for the appearance of the Newhaven women was, at least in print, confined to a connoisseurship of beauty, in which they were admired as the product of an Arcadian existence, which contrasted sharply with destitute inhabitants of Edinburgh's Old Town, or, for that matter, with any other fishing communities such as the "gin-swilling vixens of Billingsgate," the "dirty squalid fishhawkers of Dublin," or Wordsworth's "shrill and fierce" Calais fishwomen.[31] This is clearly apparent in Hugh Paton's commentary to *A Series of Original Portraits and Caricature Etchings by the Late John Kay.* In this extensive account, Paton described the women as

> Stout, clean, and blooming, if they are not the most handsome and comely of Eve's daughters, they are at least the most perfect pictures of robust and rigorous health; and not a few of them, under the pea-jacket and superabundance of petticoat with which they load themselves conceal a symmetry of form that might excite the envy of a Dutchess.[32]

Moreover, the beauty of these women might be freely observed in a Scottish version of Arcadia — the countryside between Newhaven and Edinburgh — where the connoisseur was urged to take "one of the pleasantest walks we can imagine . . . on a fine April morning [when] nature is smiling in bush and flower":

> [Here] at every turn you are sure to meet a knot of fisherwomen, fresh as the morning itself, and each with her "creel" and well filled "maun" of haddocks, or codlings, or flukes, or whitings, or skate, or lobsters, dripping from the waters of the Firth, and glistening with a freshness well calculated to tempt the eye of an epicure. A flush may be observed on the faces of the women as they bend under their load, but their step is long and elastic; and though the journey is uphill, their athletic forms appear fully able for the task.[33]

What attracted the commentator here, was not just that the women were handsome, in a healthy sort of way, but that they succeeded in being so while working very hard indeed, thereby reinforcing the commonly held opinion that hard work was good for you, or rather, them. In the case of the Newhaven and other fisherwomen, this capacity for labor was prodigious and resulted in a reputation which, by the 1860s, had reached near mythical proportions.[34]

These attitudes were not confined to Scotland, as an article in the *Art Journal* for 1887 shows.[35] This piece, part of an occasional series describing suitable subjects for painters, was an account of the fishing village of Cullercoats, situated a mile north of the river Tyne. The article — by Lillias Wassermann — is remarkably similar to the descriptions of those earlier writers on Newhaven, particularly where Wassermann came to describe the villagers and their customs. Because of their constant battle with the elements, the author remarked, the people had a look of "complete development" which

> added to their fine strong robust looks, raises them far above any other section of the working class I know.[36]

Moreover:

> Some of the fisher-lasses are very good looking indeed and even the plain ones are pleasant to look at, from their fine colour and graceful bearing. The women stoop as they grow older . . . but the young ones have generally fine upright figures, and splendid heads of hair, which, save in very rough weather, they leave uncovered.

Wassermann was also impressed, as the Newhaven commentators had been, by the ability of the Cullercoats people to "retain their

Cat. 52 *Lady Elizabeth (Rigby) Eastlake*

Fig. 3 SIR CHARLES LOCK EASTLAKE
Mrs. Charles H. Bellenden Ker
as an Italian Contadina
1835
oil on canvas
76.2 × 63.5 cm
Collection: The Tate Gallery, London, England.

peculiar characteristics, while places and things about them changed continually."[37]

The attractive and lively literary accounts of handsome, hard-working fisherfolk (for example, Paton and Cupples), combined with Hill and Adamson's visual record in the Newhaven calotypes, also represented another mid-nineteenth century phenomenon. This was the appropriation of elements of traditional peasant dress by the Victorian fashion industry, and its adaptation for wear by the upper classes. Much was made of traditionally dressed working women, whose appearance contrasted sharply with the elaborate costumes and delicate constitutions affected by women of the upper classes. In *Dress as a Fine Art* published in 1854, Mrs. Merrifield, an early exponent of a freer form of dress for women, attacked the fashion for tight lacing and recommended instead:

> The costume of the modern Greeks [i.e. peasants], which adapts itself well to the figure, the movements of which it does not restrain.[38]

These comments were accompanied by illustrations of *Peasants from the Environs of Athens* and *Shepherdesses of Arcadia*, which were taken from de Stacklenberg's *Costumes of the Peoples of Ancient Greece* published in 1826.

Mrs. Merrifield was also critical of the fashion for wearing low cut dresses (cat. 52) upon which, she argued somewhat unconvincingly, "men look . . . with unmitigated distaste."[39] Instead she recommended that

> the bust should be covered after the modest and becoming fashion of the Italian [peasant] women, whose highly picturesque costume painters are so fond of representing.[40]

She then cited as examples of this style: Sir Charles Eastlake's *Pilgrims in Sight of Rome* and Lehman's *The Grape Gatherers of Capri*, both of which were illustrated in the *Art Journal* for 1848. While this issue of the magazine appeared three years after the Newhaven calotypes were made, the taste for peasant dress among the upper classes had already been established for some time. Eastlake's *Pilgrims* was painted in 1827 and his portrait of *Mrs. Charles H. Bellenden Ker as an Italian Contadina* (of which Lady Eastlake claimed "he could have filled his hands with this class of occupation") was completed in 1835 (fig. 3).[41]

A taste for traditional types of British rural costume emerged shortly afterwards, when a modified version of the fisherwomen's outfit — made of silks rather than coarser materials — was adapted for fashionable women, probably for wearing at the new seaside resorts. This fashion, as well as the contrasting physical attributes and the real and make-believe fisherwives, was humorously reflected in George du Maurier's cartoon for *Punch* in 1871, which was captioned:

"Fact or fiction
 or
ye bonny fisherwives of Scarborough and their imitators" (fig. 4).

Fig. 4 *Fact or fiction*
    or
*ye bonny fisherwives of Scarborough
and their imitators.* From *Punch* cartoon
by George du Maurier.

In this context, the exotic — even "foreign" — appearance of the Newhaven women clearly attracted considerable attention. Moreover, the long-held concept of Edinburgh as the "Modern Athens" required that the city should have its own attractive, working, rural and coastal population, "pretty as so many fine living pictures" as Lady Eastlake would have it, to rival the peasants from the environs of Athens and Rome, whom Eastlake and Lehman had painted with such success in the preceding years. In the case of Edinburgh, this requirement was all the more important because the working-class inhabitants of the historic Old Town could, by no stretch of the imagination, qualify as exotic. Instead, that part of the city had declined into such deplorable conditions of poverty and deprivation that philanthropists and the city authorities were driven to take urgent action in the 1850s and 1860s.[42] Indeed, when photographers like Hill and Adamson, Thomas Keith (1827-1885) and Archibald Burns (active 1858-1880) did venture to work in the area, their interest was largely confined to the picturesque buildings, while the densely crowded slum population, referred to in all the city reports, was banished or confined to the background shadows.[43] There the ragged appearance of the beggars, prostitutes and criminals who lived in the narrow, unsanitary closes would not spoil the view or offend the sensibilities of the photographer's audience. By comparison, the Newhaven women must have seemed a particularly appropriate appendage to the "Modern Athens," an awareness which was confirmed by Dr. John Brown's remarks on Hill and Adamson's two calotypes of Mrs. Elizabeth Hall and another fishwife in *The Witness*, published in Edinburgh on 22 April 1846:

> These clean, sonsy, caller, comely, substantial fishwives, what a comely sight! . . . As easy, as unconfined, as deep bosomed and ample, as any Greek matron. Indeed we have often been struck, when seeing them sitting together around their oyster creels, with their likeness to those awful and majestic women, the Fates of the Elgin marbles, the casts of which are in the Gallery of the Royal Institution.[44]

Nevertheless, polite society was often suspicious of the working garb of the fisherwomen, and particularly their shocking habit of exposing their legs. That this was a necessity, dictated by their occupation, does not appear to have bothered those who made the rules in these matters, and the taboo against a respectable woman exposing so much as a glimmer of an ankle provoked a great deal of prudish censure, as George du Maurier's *Punch* cartoon of French fisherwomen at Boulogne revealed (fig. 5). According to another

Fig. 5 *"Honi Soit"*
Anne and Sarah see some Fishwomen 'clothed
that indelicate that you might have knocked
them down with a feather' (Boulogne). From
Punch cartoon by George du Maurier, 1866.

Punch article of 1851, the reputation of these young Frenchwomen attracted a rather different response from young Englishmen who apparently

> take much pleasure to regard [the young fisherwomen's legs] all the day at Dieppe and Boulogne.[45]

Arthur Munby, an inveterate observer of working-class life, also visited Boulogne and his diary account of the fisherwomen's activities provides an interesting example of the way in which the term "picturesque" could be stretched to sublimate what his contemporaries might have called his "baser instincts":

> How picturesque they looked [Munby wrote] stooped under their baskets, and strolling in regular beat along the sunny sands! And when they came to a landlocked pool, the pack would plunge in, delighting in the cool water, and lifting their scanty kilts to the hips showing a white thigh strangely different from the sunburnt leg below.[46]

Nearer home, similar activities by the bait gatherers of St. Andrews were banned by Provost Playfair (or "playfoul" as he became known) on moral grounds. Even the Newhaven fishwives did not escape censure later in the century, when it was suggested, as mentioned earlier, that some women took advantage of their fish hawking in Edinburgh to supplement their earnings in an immoral manner. However, if Hill and Adamson were familiar with these reputedly negative aspects of Newhaven life, they once again took care to avoid any emphasis which would detract from the Arcadian atmosphere of bucolic, hard-working fisherfolk, which was also characteristic of the literary and historical commentators on Scottish life.[47]

Hill and Adamson's Newhaven calotypes represent some of the earliest attempts to make use of the images of traditionally dressed working people for possible commercial gain. Indeed, their work closely resembles the early tourist photographs of peasant women taken by Joseph James Forrester at Ninho in northern Portugal.[48] Following Hill and Adamson's lead, other Edinburgh photographers took up the subject of the Newhaven fishwives, whom they now photographed using the faster collodion process, against often incongruous backdrops in their studios.[49] As tourism expanded in Scotland, the Newhaven women became the standard representation of the historic working-class trades of old Edinburgh, for example, in *Macara's Series of Scottish Photographs*, where they appeared alongside another popular series on *Scotch Washing*.[50]

Not all the photographs of "fishwives" taken in the later years of the nineteenth century were of the real residents of Newhaven. By the 1880s, the fishwives' costume had been appropriated as a

24

popular item of fancy dress by some middle-class households. Similarly, female tourists frequently donned the fishwives' outfit at the photographer's as a suitably picturesque counterpart to male Highland attire. Thus, Murray and Campbell, photographers, of 68 Princes Street, Edinburgh, between 1877 and 1891, advertised "Ladies Photographed in fishwife Dress and Gentlemen in Highland Dress. Dresses for the above styles kept on the premises."[51] In these circumstances of commercial exploitation, it was usually left to talented amateurs, like James Crighton, to photograph the Newhaven fisherfolk in the sympathetic manner first accorded them by David Octavius Hill and Robert Adamson.

ACKNOWLEDGEMENTS

I am extremely grateful to Sara Stevenson and to Julie Lawson of the Scottish National Portrait Gallery for sharing their insights on the work of Hill and Adamson with me. K.B.

NOTES

1. For example, Barrell, John: *The dark side of the landscape: the rural poor in English painting 1730-1840.* Cambridge, C.U.P., 1985.

2. There are some exceptions, e.g. Sekula, Alan, "Photography Between Labour and Capital," in Buchloh, Benjamin H.D., and Robert Wilkie (eds.), *Mining Photographs and Other Pictures 1948-1968, A Selection from the Shedden Studio, Glace Bay, Cape Breton.* (Halifax: The Press of the Nova Scotia College of Art and Design; Sydney: The University College of Cape Breton Press): 193-268.

3. Strong, Roy and Colin Ford: *An Early Victorian Album. The Photographic Masterpieces (1843-1847) of David Octavius Hill and Robert Adamson.* (New York: Alfred A. Knopf, Inc., 1976): 36-37.

4. Paton, Hugh. *A Series of Original Portraits and Caricature Etchings by the Late John Kay, Miniature Painter, Edinburgh; with Biographical Sketches and Illustrative Anecdotes,* 2 vols. (Edinburgh, Hugh Paton, Head Horse Wynde, and Smith Elder and Co., London, 1838): 338-345.

5. As John Taylor remarked in *Life and Landscape: P.H. Emerson Art and Photography . . .,* the apprehension of class can be extremely subtle, and eludes quantitative analysis" (p. 74). However, a class map of England made in 1867 divided the upper and middle classes and the laboring classes into two groups "which stood to each other in the ratio 1:4" (Taylor, p. 74).

6. For early histories of Newhaven see Dempster, Henry: *History of Newhaven: showing where founded; its rise, progress and the cause for its decline . . .* Glasgow, Aird and Coghill, 1870; Cupples, Mrs. G.: *Newhaven, its origin and history.* Edinburgh, T. and A. Constable, 1888. The most recent account is McGowran, Tom: *Newhaven-on-Forth. Port of Grace.* Edinburgh, John Donald Publishers Ltd., 1985.

7. The Edinburgh, Leith and Granton Railway (or Edinburgh, Leith and Newhaven Railway as it was known until at least 1839) opened in 1842.

8. Apart from the successful activities of the Rev. Dr. Chalmers (cat. 68), the main debate was conducted by Henry Dempster, the "Old Voyager," in his pamphlet: *History of Newhaven: showing where founded; its rise, progress, and the cause for its decline. With suggestions how to prevent further decay, and again resussitate the ancient village.* Glasgow: Aird and Coghill, 1870. Creel hawking survived until the 1950s.

9. Both referred to by Sara Stevenson in her essay "Robert Adamson and David Octavius Hill" in the exhibition catalogue *Printed Light.* (Edinburgh, Scottish National Portrait Gallery and HMSO, 1986): 163.

10. McGowran, Tom. *Newhaven-on-Forth. Port of Grace.* Edinburgh, John Donald Publishers Ltd., 1985, ch. 1.

11. Published in Edinburgh, 1892, p. 75.

12. op. cit. Cupples, p. 16.

13. ibid. Cupples, p. 20.

14. op. cit. Paton, p. 343

15. Published in House of Lords Papers, 1842, vol. 28.

16. Cockburn remarked in his diary: "The man must be very blind who does not see the shadow of the popular tree is enlarging and darkening." Quoted by Smout, T.C. *A Century of the Scottish People 1830-1950.* (London, Collins, 1986): 7-8.

17. For a study of the Chartists, see Wilson, A. *The Chartist Movement in Scotland,* Manchester, 1970.

18. op. cit. Paton, pp. 338-339.

19. See: Thompson, E.P. *The Making of the English Working Class.* Pelican Books, 1986. Chapter 6, "Exploitation."

20. *Quarterly Review.* Vol. 79, no. 158, pp. 372-399.

21. ibid. pp. 386-387.

22. Quoted by Errington, L. in *Tribute to Wilkie from the National Gallery of Scotland . . .* (Edinburgh, The National Galleries of Scotland, 1985): 14.

23. Quoted in: *Journals and Correspondence of Lady Eastlake edited by her nephew Charles Eastlake Smith,* 2 vols, (London, John Murray, 1895): 183.

24. op cit. *Quarterly Review,* "The Art of Dress," p. 387.

25. op. cit. Barrell, Introduction.

26. Quoted by Barrell, p. 102; painting reproduced p. 112.

27. For a discussion of the social implications of the painting and the quotation, see Duncan Macmillan, *Painting in Scotland, The Golden Age,* (Oxford, Phaidon Press, 1986): 166-169.

28. For example, the *Gazetteer of Scotland* for 1832 remarked: "The village [Newhaven] . . . remains in its pristine condition, and is certainly one of the dirtiest places in Scotland." Quoted by John Burnett in "Day Return to Newhaven." *The Bulletin of the Scottish Society for the History of Photography,* Spring, 1986, p. 29. See also Provost Playfair's attempts to clean up St. Andrews in "Hill and Adamson at St. Andrews: The Fishergate Calotypes" by Graham Smith in *Print Collector's Newsletter,* vol. XII, no. 2, May-June 1981, pp. 33-37.

29. See *An Inquiry into Destitution, Prostitution and Crime in Edinburgh,* Edinburgh, Bertram and Co., 1851.

30. For example, Henry Dempster suggested that if the fishwives lost their business to the fishmongers, one "material advantage" would be that they might "remain at home . . . looking after the children's instruction and husband's comforts . . . .", p. 7.

31. Quoted by Paton, p. 339. Paton admits that the Newhaven women are inclined to "dram-drinking" but not to drunkenness.

32. ibid. Paton, p. 338.

33. ibid. Paton, p. 339.

34. According to the *Statistical Account for Scotland,* the women often carried loads of 150 pounds and more. One group of three was said to have carried (in relays) a load of 200 pounds from Dunbar to Edinburgh, a distance of twenty-seven miles in five hours. Quoted by Paton, pp. 339-340.

35. Wassermann, Lillias. "Some Fisher Folk," pp. 57-60.

36. ibid. Wassermann, p. 58.

37. ibid. p. 58.

38. Published in London by Arthur Hall, Virtue, & Co., 1854, p. 14. Mrs. Merrifield was an Hon. Member of the Academy of Fine Arts, Bologna; author of *The Ancient Practise of Painting* and *The Art of Fresco Painting.* Merrifield objected to the artificial constrictions of fashionable dress: "The athletic — if the term may be applied to females — form of the country girl would appear ridiculous with the small waist, and the white taper fingers and small feet of the individuals who come under the denomination of slender forms" (p. 25).

39. ibid. p. 13.

40. ibid. p. 14.

41. Lady Eastlake. *Memoir of Eastlake* (in *Contributions to the Literature of the Fine Arts,* 1870) pp. 146 and 195.

42. See: *An Inquiry into Destitition, Prostitution and Crime in Edinburgh.* Edinburgh, Bertram and Co., 1851. In Ch.1, the Inquiry reported: "At our very doors, crawling about our streets, lanes, and closes, to beg or to steal, we have a population of thousands whose ignorance is only equalled by their utter destitution . . .". The area of Halkerstone's Wynde (Ch.1) was found to be a "rookery of thieves and prostitutes of the very lowest description. The dens — for houses we could not designate them — . . . were some of them in a fearfully dilapidated condition, and looked as if they would have shaken to the earth by the least breath of a storm."

43. Archibald Burns published a book called *Picturesque Bits* in 1868, containing his own photographs of the Old Town of Edinburgh.

44. Quoted by Stevenson in *Printed Light* p. 154.

45. Quoted by Michael Hiley in *Victorian Working Women: Portraits from Life* (London, Gordon Fraser, 1979): 37.

46. ibid., p. 37.

47. Several ideas in this essay have been developed from a paper entitled *The Newhaven Calotypes of D.O. Hill and Robert Adamson,* which I gave at the Scottish National Portrait Gallery on 14th August 1986 as part of the *Printed Light Lectures.*

48. See for example, Forrester's work in the Scottish National Portrait Gallery: PGP 56(4); PGP 56(7).

49. See for example, a hand-colored *carte-de-visite* of a fishergirl by James Ross, 90 Princes Street, Edinburgh. Collection, Scottish National Portrait Gallery.

50. Both in collection Scottish National Portrait Gallery. The series on *Scotch Washing* shows country women treading the washing in tubs beside a stream.

51. Collection Scottish National Portrait Gallery. I am grateful to Sara Stevenson for bringing this item to my attention.

Sketches In Brown: The Portrait Photography Of David Octavius Hill And Robert Adamson

David Harris

The origins of Hill and Adamson's partnership are well known and may be summarized briefly. David Octavius Hill (1802-1870), a landscape painter and secretary of the Royal Scottish Academy, was one of the witnesses to the Disruption of the Church of Scotland on May 18, 1843, which led to the establishment of the Free Church. Hill set out to commemorate the event in a large historical painting depicting the participants. Sir David Brewster, the physicist who introduced the calotype to Scotland, suggested that Hill employ Robert Adamson (1821-1848), who had recently opened a photographic studio in Edinburgh, to make studies of the figures to be included in the painting. From this initial venture grew a partnership that was to last the five years until Adamson's early death in 1848. During this period, they made approximately three thousand photographs. In addition to the vast number of portraits, Hill and Adamson produced architectural, landscape and genre photographs. It is with the portraiture that this essay is concerned.

One of the earliest accounts of the portraits by Hill and Adamson is perhaps one of the most illuminating. Hugh Miller, the editor of *The Witness*, wrote of their work in the July 12, 1843, issue:

> Here, for instance, is a portrait exactly after the manner of Raeburn. There is the same broad freedom of touch; no nice miniature stipplings, as if laid in by the point of a needle — no sharp-edged strokes: all is solid, massy, broad; more distinct at a distance than when viewed near at hand. The arrangement of the lights and shadows seems rather the result of a happy haste, in which half the effect was produced by design, half by accident, than of great labour and care; and yet how exquisitely true the general aspect! Every stroke tells, and serves, as in the portraits of Raeburn, to do more than relieve the features: it serves also to indicate the prevailing mood and predominant power to the mind. And here is another portrait, quiet, deeply-toned, gentlemanly, — a transcript apparently of one of the more characteristic portraits of Sir Thomas Lawrence. Perhaps, however, of all our British artists, the artist whose published works most nearly resemble a set of these drawings is Sir Joshua Reynolds. We have a folio volume of engravings from his pictures before us; and when, placing side by side with the prints the sketches in brown, we remark the striking similarity of style that prevails between them, we feel more strongly than at perhaps any former period, that the friend of Johnson and of Burke must have been a consummate master of his art.[1]

This passage has been quoted at length since it reveals at once how a contemporary responded to the portraits. In common with other initial reactions to photography, Miller relied upon a familiar vocabulary and drew upon well-known painters for his comparisons. His description of the photographs as ''drawings'' and ''sketches in brown'' and his contention that the photographs were superior to mezzotint engravings would have made the nature of portrait photography clear to his readers by emphasizing those visual qualities common to other tonal and monochromatic media.

Furthermore, in writing that the portraits were "exactly after the manner of Raeburn," a "transcript . . . of one of the more characteristic portraits" of Lawrence and "resemble[d]" engravings after Reynolds, Miller has situated them firmly within a tradition. Rather than stressing how the photographs marked a break with a prevailing portrait tradition (which has been the case in twentieth century writing),[2] he celebrated what he saw as a continuity. Such an argument had a double purpose: the painted portraits were bestowed retrospectively with a "photographic" truthfulness while they, in turn, conferred upon the photographs an artistic legitimacy.

The general purpose of Miller's position is clear — the photographic portraits developed from within a painting tradition — but upon close examination, it reveals inconsistencies and lapses in logic. While under certain circumstances salted paper prints, drawings and mezzotint engravings share some visual characteristics, Miller has conveniently, if only inadvertently, ignored others such as color, scale and method of working, which would have made such comparisons less convincing. Equally, Miller's argument over the apparent truthfulness of the painted portraits is confusing. Certainly one can argue that Hill and Adamson based their portraits on the work of earlier painters, but to suggest that these painters had striven towards the kind of realism and appearance that the later photographs represented is, at the very least, illogical. Furthermore, his references to the painted portraits lack specificity: one would like to see the prints in his portfolio which he used for his comparisons. It is not difficult to find portraits by Reynolds, Lawrence and Raeburn that are quite unlike those of the photographers; even Raeburn's works, with which almost every commentator has compared the work of Hill and Adamson, reveal a range and variety that would limit such comparisons to specific and qualified instances.[3] Moreover, it is not clear whether Miller is suggesting that Hill and Adamson modelled their work deliberately on particular portraits or on stylistic conventions from this tradition.

Miller's text is of far greater interest as an early and enthusiastic response to the portraits of Hill and Adamson than as a sound, well-constructed argument. More importantly, it identifies the critical tradition within which the author operated. If one reads through academic writings on portraiture, Miller's position becomes clear. The belief that art was the ideal imitation of nature had provided the substance of British academic theory since the middle of the eighteenth century.[4] "Ideal nature" meant that representations should not copy nature too closely or minutely but rather, through a process of selection and generalization, portray it in an ideal state beyond that of mere appearance.[5] As well, the "ideal" was embodied in the acknowledged masterpieces from the past — notably in Greek and Roman sculpture and in Renaissance painting. The contemporary artist was taught to think of the past as supplying the tradition from which one would derive compositional principles and even poses, and as the standard against which one's work would be measured.[6]

Although the theory had been developed principally to support history painting, it also affected the way that portraiture was conceived. The portrait painter, in dealing with individuals, had to strike a delicate balance between producing a convincing likeness and yet presenting a more generalized impression of the person. In his *Discourses on Art*, Sir Joshua Reynolds wrote:

> The excellence of Portrait-Painting, and we may add even the likeness, the character, and countenance . . . depend more upon the general effect produced by the painter, than on the exact expression of the peculiarities, or minute discrimination of the parts.[7]

By "general effect," Reynolds clearly meant the total impression that a person and, consequently, his portrait produces. In another discussion about the sketchlike painting technique of Sir Thomas Gainsborough, Reynolds argued that the painter's technique enhanced the sense of a vibrant personality, rather than diminished it:

> It is presupposed that in this undetermined manner there is the general effect; enough to remind the spectator of the original; the imagination supplies the rest, and perhaps more satisfactorily to himself, if not more exactly, than the artist, with all his care, could possibly have done.[8]

Although written in the eighteenth century, Reynolds' *Discourses* provided the basis for most British writing on art during the first half of the nineteenth century. These ideas and even his use of language are found in the passage quoted from Miller's article. Phrases such as "All is solid, massy, broad; more distinct at a distance than when viewed near at hand" and that the portraits "indicate the prevailing mood and predominant power of the mind" find an echo in Reynolds' writings.

Presumably, David Octavius Hill was equally, if not more, familiar with this tradition than Miller. As secretary of the Royal Scottish Academy, he was responsible for securing paintings for the annual exhibition. Through his brother Alexander, who operated a print shop in Edinburgh, he would have been familiar with mezzotint engravings after the work of painters such as Raeburn, Lawrence and Reynolds.[9] Lacking substantial statements from the photographers themselves, one can infer their aesthetic ambitions from evidence of their working methods and from the actual photographs. The writings of such essayists as Hugh Miller[10] and instruction found in contemporary photography treatises and manuals provide additional information on both the aesthetic considerations and technical practices of Hill and Adamson.

Cat. 27 *John Ban Mackenzie*

Cat. 48 *Miss Crampton*

Cat. 54 *Mrs. Kinloch*

As a result of relatively insensitive negatives and long exposures, all the portraits were made out-of-doors, the majority of them in the sheltered garden of Rock House on Calton Hill in Edinburgh. While the setting is not always apparent, it is evident in the backgrounds of such portraits as John Ban Mackenzie (cat. 27) and the portrait of Miss Crampton (cat. 48). Exposures varied from ten seconds to three minutes, depending on both the time of day and the time of year.[11] In order to help the sitters maintain their poses, headrests were invariably used: evidence of this device can be seen in the portrait of an unknown man (possibly Captain Martin, cat. 42).[12] In addition, a variety of poses, which allowed the sitters to steady their arms on tables, armrests of chairs, and large books, was selected. The portraits of Mrs. Kinloch (cat. 54) and James Nasmyth (cat. 33) are representative of this practice. Since the portrait lenses allowed for only a relatively limited area to be in focus, poses were compressed into shallow space.[13] Consequently the sitter's arms and legs were kept close to the plane of the body so as to prevent them from being out of focus and appearing unnaturally large and distorted.[14]

While the technicalities of the cameras and the other photographic materials restricted Hill and Adamson, their portraiture shows how successfully they adapted traditional poses and narrative conventions to the new working conditions.

In a letter to the painter David Roberts in March 1845, Hill indicated that he was responsible for the artistic direction and positioning of the sitters while Adamson handled the cameras and the chemistry.[15] Hill's standard approach was to place his sitters in direct sunlight before an open doorway so that the line of the head, shoulders, arms and torso separated the figure clearly from the dark background.[16] The sitter emerged dramatically, with a strong physical presence. Curtains, open trelliswork, tables with books, vases and small statues provided decorative relief and filled out the occupational and domestic narratives.

There is considerable evidence of the care with which Hill arranged the poses and decorative details. In the same letter to Roberts, Hill wrote that "the arrangement of the picture is as much an effort of the artist as if he was in reality going to paint it."[17] Slight shifts in orientation between the head, the limbs and body create a sense of animation and even spontaneity in a pose that had been held for a considerable length of time. In the portrait of Anna Jameson (cat. 53), the turning of her head, the creases in the fabric of her dress and the turbulent swirl of fabric surrounding her left arm are suggestive of a willful and dynamic personality. Alternatively, in the portrait of Reverend Alexander Keith (cat. 22), the gentle cascade of drapery and the positioning of his hands upon the heavy volumes infuse the photograph with a quiet and meditative calm.

The central uncertainty in Miller's text may never be entirely resolved. The extent to which Hill and Adamson based their portraits on specific precedents or general conventions of a portrait tradition is only part of a complex situation. That their portraits were modelled on those of Raeburn may well be deliberate and conscious (as the writings of Reynolds had sanctioned, to a degree); equally, the properties of salted paper prints and, in the case of Raeburn, the conditions under which he worked, contributed to the similarities found between the two different media.

Raeburn's studio at York Place, Edinburgh, was a large rectangular room, fifty-five feet long, forty-five feet wide and fourteen feet high; the subject was seated on a raised platform directly beneath a skylight.[18] Dr. John Brown described Raeburn's method of painting as follows:

> Placing his sitter on the pedestal, he looked at him from the other end of a long room, gazing at him intently with his great dark eyes. Having got the idea of the man, what of him carried farthest and 'told', he walked hastily up to the canvas, never looking at his sitter, and put down what he had fixed in his inner eye; he then withdrew again, took another gaze and recorded its result, and so on, making no measurements.[19]

As a consequence of this practice, Raeburn's portraits are broadly painted and, because of the overhead lighting, show areas of strong light and dark shadow (see fig. 1).

The use of paper as the support for both photographic negatives and positives produced very similar effects to those achieved by Raeburn. In a salted paper print, the image is embedded within the fibers of the paper, thereby softening outlines and details, and massing light and dark areas.[20] Furthermore, the appearance and coloration of salted paper prints (in contrast to those of daguerreotypes) coincided with contemporary English taste.[21] A reviewer of William Henry Fox Talbot's *The Pencil of Nature* (which also included salted paper prints) detailed this preference:

> The neutral tints are of warm brownish hue, with occasionally a tinge of red or purple; the tint different in every instance, its hue depending on the chemical operation of light on the paper. This variation of tint is rather pleasing than otherwise; for all the varieties are mellow and agreeable to the eye, and much preferable to the metallic glare and livid blackness of the Daguerreotype-plates.[22]

In spite of an allegiance to the painted portrait tradition, photographic portraiture did represent a departure from previous forms of representation. What distinguished the photographs finally was their direct connection with the subject which the optical and chemical processes seemed to guarantee. Writing in 1843, Sir David Brewster set out the position:

Cat. 33 *James Nasmyth*

Fig. 1 SIR HENRY RAEBURN
Portrait of William Darnell
oil on canvas
128.3 × 102.2 cm
Collection: Art Gallery of Ontario,
Toronto Canada.

33

The photograph is connected with its prototype by sensibilities peculiarly touching. It was the very light which radiated from his brow — the identical gleam which lighted up his eye — the pallid hue which hung upon his cheek — that pencilled the cherished image, and fixed themselves for ever there.[23]

This point was also made by Hugh Miller in his 1843 essay on Hill and Adamson. In a passage in which the author compared an engraving to a salted paper print of Dr. Thomas Chalmers, he emphasized the "truthful" superiority of the latter:

> There is truth, breadth, and power about [the salted paper print] which we find in only the highest walks of art, and not often in these. We have placed a head of Dr. Chalmers taken in this way beside one of the most powerful prints of him yet given to the public, and find from the contrast that the latter, with all its power, is but a mere approximation. There is a *skinniness* about the lips which is not true to nature; the chin is not brought strongly enough out; the shade beneath the under lip is too broad and too flat; the nose droops, and lacks the firm-set appearance so characteristic of the original; and while the breadth of the forehead is exaggerated there is scarce justice done to its height. We decide at once in favour of the calotype — it is truth itself.[24]

The appeal and authority of the work of Hill and Adamson for Miller lay precisely in what he perceived as its dual adherence to a previous portrait tradition as represented by the work of Reynolds, Lawrence and Raeburn — and to a fidelity to appearances that was possible only with the photographic camera. These two ideas now seem quite separate; that Miller was able to bring them together reveals a great deal about the artistic climate of Scotland in the 1840s. A contemporary's perception of the portraits of Hill and Adamson may be as close as we are likely to come to a sense of what the work represented at the time when they were made.

ACKNOWLEDGEMENTS

I would like to acknowledge the gracious help of Nigel Thorp and Sara Stevenson at their respective institutions, John Gifford and Tristram Clarke in the research on my catalogue entry on the panorama, and particularly Linda Eerme for all her help and support during the writing of my essay. D.H.

NOTES

1. *The Witness*, 12 July 1843. The article was reprinted in Hugh Miller's *Leading Articles on Various Subjects*, ed. Rev. J. Davidson, 5th ed. (Edinburgh: William P. Nimmo, 1873), 186.

2. See, for example, Paul Strand, "Photography and the New God," *Broom*, 3 (1923): 252-258; reprinted in Nathan Lyons, ed., *Photographers on Photography* (Englewood Cliffs, N.J.: Prentice Hall, 1966), 139-140.

3. Several comparisons are illustrated in Roy Strong, "D.O. Hill and the Academic Tradition" in Colin Ford, ed., *An Early Victorian Album: The Photographic Masterpieces (1843-1847) of David Octavius Hill and Robert Adamson* (New York, N.Y.: Alfred A. Knopf, 1976), 52-53.

4. An excellent discussion of this tradition is found in Rensselaer W. Lee, *Ut Pictura Poesis: The Humanistic Theory of Painting* (New York, N.Y.: W.W. Norton & Co., 1967). Sir Joshua Reynolds' *Discourses on Art*, delivered between 1769-1790, provided a full articulation of this theory. On Reynolds' ideas, see Walter J. Hipple, "General and Particular in the Discourses of Sir Joshua Reynolds: A Study of Method," *The Journal of Aesthetics and Art Criticism*, 11 (1953): 231-247.

5. Sir Joshua Reynolds, *Discourses on Art*, Robert R. Wark, ed. (San Marino, Calif.: Huntington Library, 1959), 44.

6. Reynolds, *Discourses*, 100-101; see also 184-185.

7. Reynolds, *Discourses*, 200.

8. Reynolds, *Discourses*, 259.

9. This idea was first suggested by Heinrich Schwarz in his *David Octavius Hill: Master of Photography*, trans. H.E. Fraenkel (New York, N.Y.: Viking Press, 1931), 39. Schwarz argues that salted paper prints and mezzotint engravings are both tonal media in which an "unbroken continuity from brightest light to darkest shadow" is recorded. (p. 38). Hence mezzotints provided Hill with a visual precedent for their portraits:

> In [Hill and Adamson's] work, as in mezzotints, light separates itself reluctantly from shadow. Soft half-tones, emerging from deepest shade, temper the transition to the bright spots of heads and hands. As in the mezzotint, a fluent chiaroscuro plays about the bodies and fuses the figures and the space about them into a harmonious unity. And again, as in the mezzotint, one can actually feel the surface textures in cravats of shimmering satin, waistcoats of dull-glowing velvet, collars of thick fur, and shawls made of soft Scottish wool. (p. 39).

10. Given the date of Miller's article, July 12, 1843, one month after the beginning of Hill and Adamson's collaboration, one must assume that much of the information dealing with the photographic process and its aesthetic applications was supplied by the photographers themselves. Hill and Adamson photographed Miller several times: for portraits of Hugh Miller, see cat. 29 in the present exhibition and Sara Stevenson, *David Octavius Hill and Robert Adamson: Catalogue of their calotypes taken between 1843 and 1847 in the collection of the Scottish National Portrait Gallery* (Edinburgh: Trustees of the National Galleries of Scotland, 1981), 91.

11. These times are taken from Sir David Brewster's originally anonymously published account of photographic processes. See Sir David Brewster, "Photogenic Drawings, or Drawings by the Agency of Light," *The Edinburgh Review*, 77 (1843):167:

> The time of impressing the paper with an *invisible* image, varies from *ten seconds* to several minutes, according to the intensity of the light. In the light of a summer sun from *ten* to *fifty* seconds will be sufficient; but when the sun is not strong, *two* or *three* minutes in summer is necessary.

At the end of the period covered by Hill and Adamson's partnership, similar figures are provided in Henry Snelling, *The History and Practice of the Art of Photography; or The Production of Pictures Through the Agency of Light* (New York, N.Y.: G.P. Putnam, 1849), 100:

> *Time of Exposure*. With regard to the time which should be allowed for the paper to remain in the camera, no direct rules can be laid down; this will depend altogether on the nature of the object to be copied, and the light which prevails. All that can be said is that the time necessary for forming a good picture varies from thirty seconds to five minutes, and it will be naturally the first object of the operator to gain by experience this important knowledge.

12. A typical headrest is illustrated in the exhibition catalogue, Katherine Michaelson, *A Centenary Exhibition of the Works of David Octavius Hill 1802-1870 and Robert Adamson 1821-1848* (Edinburgh: Scottish Arts Council, 1970), pl. 4. A description appears on page 78. For a contemporary account of the necessity of using a headrest, see Nöel-Marie-Paymal Lerebours, *A Treatise on Photography*, trans. J. Egerton (London: Longman, Brown, Green and Longmans, 1843), 67.

13. On portrait lenses, see Brian Coe, *Cameras: From Daguerreotypes to Instant Pictures* (New York, N.Y.: Crown Publishers, 1978), 189-190.

14. Contemporary manuals discussed the effects of short focus lenses on portraiture. For example, Lerebours in his *Treatise on Photography*, p.68 wrote:

> all parts of the figure should be as near as possible equidistant from the object glass. The legs should be turned sideways, in order to avoid giving undue proportions to the feet and the knees. For the same reason, the hands should not be advanced too far from the body, or they would appear enormously large.

For later but similar discussions of this problem, see Phillip H. Delamotte, *The Practice of Photography: A Manual for Students and Amateurs*, 2nd ed. (London: Photographic Institution, 1855), 9 and 12, and William Lake Price, *A Manual of Photographic Manipulation, Treating the Practice of the Art and its Various Applications to Nature*, 2nd ed. (London: John Churchill & Son, 1868), 86-87 and 157-159.

15. The letter is published in Sara Stevenson, "Cold buckets of ignorant criticism: Qualified success in the partnership of David Octavius Hill and Robert Adamson," *The Photographic Collector*, 4 (1983): 336-347, see particularly 336-339. The exact nature of their collaboration has been the subject of much discussion. In a statement such as appeared in the Royal Scottish Academy catalogue of 1845, "Calotype Portrait Sketches, designed and arranged by D.O. Hill and executed by R. Adamson", the division of labor and responsibility seems neatly drawn. However, it has been pointed out that Hill must have had some knowledge of the photographic process and the nature of materials used in order to produce coherent images. See William Crawford, *The Keepers of Light: A History and Working Guide to Early Photographic Processes* (Dobbs Ferry, N.Y.: Morgan & Morgan, 1979), 36-37.

16. A study of the negatives and prints indicates that the former were often retouched along the shoulders, arms and through the hair of the subject to create the desired separation.

17. Stevenson, "Cold buckets": 337.

18. The description of the studio is taken from Edward Pinnington, *Sir Henry Raeburn R.A.* (London: The Walter Scott Publishing Co. Ltd. 1904), 125.

19. Pinnington, *Raeburn*, 124

20. See André Jammes and Eugene Parry Janis, *The Art of French Calotype* (Princeton, N.J.: Princeton University Press, 1983), 9-12.

21. See Stevenson, *David Octavius Hill and Robert Adamson*, 22 and Stevenson, "Cold buckets": 343.

22. *The Spectator*, 838 (July 20, 1844): 685.

23. Brewster, "Photogenic Drawings": 170.

24. Miller, *Leading Articles*, 183. See also Anon, "Dr. Chalmers' Posthumous Works" *The North British Review*, 8 (Nov. 1847-Feb. 1848): 398-399.

Cat. 128 *Fence and Trees in Colinton Wood*

Cat. 122 *The Mound, Edinburgh*

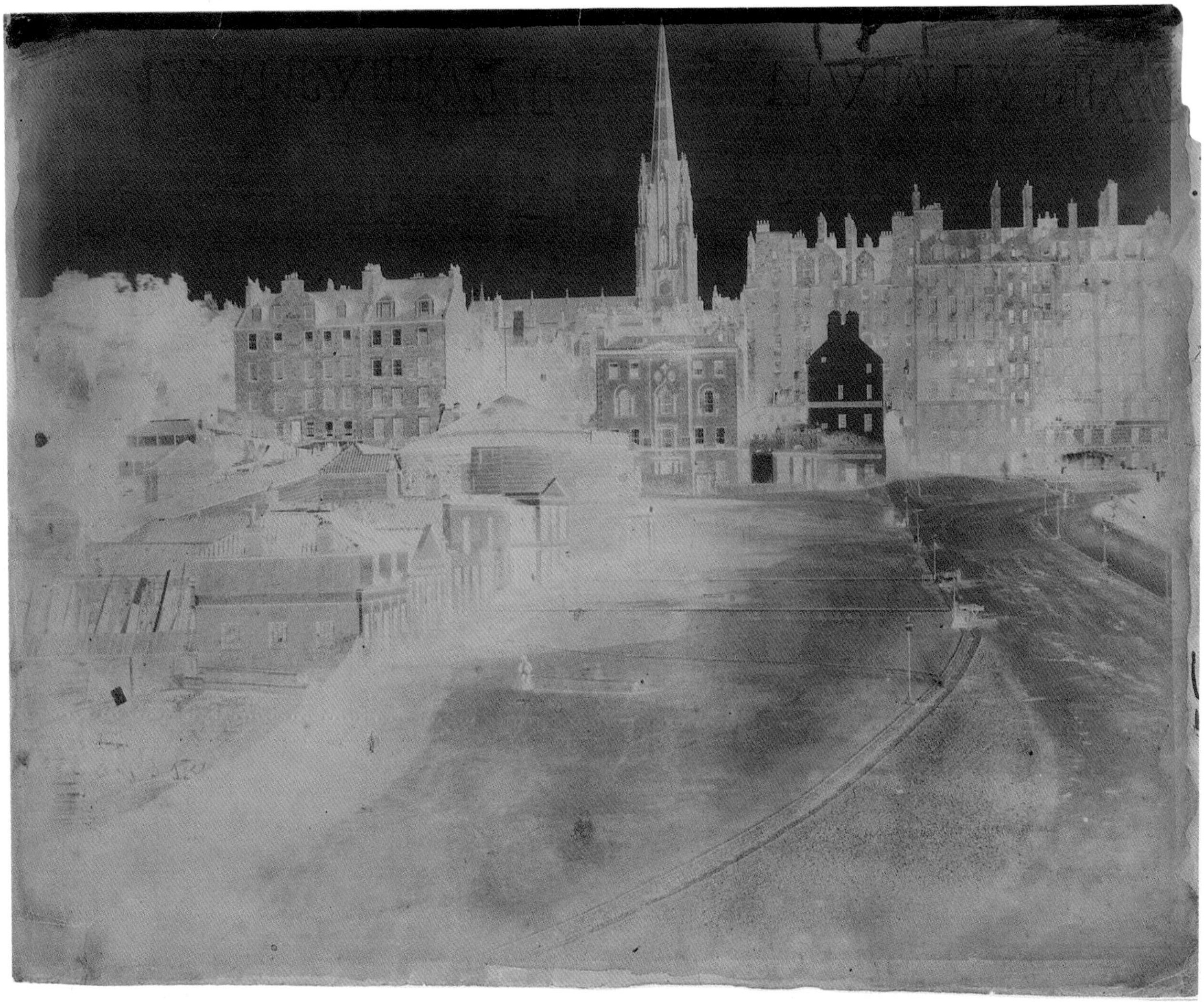

The Calotype And The Work Of Hill And Adamson

Grant Arnold

David Octavius Hill (1802-1870) and Robert Adamson (1821-1848) are counted among the first artists to exploit successfully the possibilities of photography, for their collaboration began only four years after details of the first photographic processes were made public in 1839. The invention of photography has often been viewed as the beginning of radical change in the European tradition of pictorial representation. However, many early photographers, who consciously placed their work in a fine art context, produced images which conformed fairly closely to existing pictorial conventions. For the most part, these photographers, Hill and Adamson included, chose to work with the paper-based calotype process. It will be useful, within the context of this exhibition, to summarize the origins of some of the earliest photographic processes and to examine the specific properties of the calotype in relation to Hill and Adamson's work.

During the early decades of the nineteenth century, a number of scientists and inventors were attempting to develop a process which would, through the use of light-sensitive chemical compounds, make permanent the image formed by light in a camera obscura. Each had taken a different approach to the problem and, until January 1839, each was unaware of the others' experiments. Of at least three processes which had more or less been perfected by the 1840s, two, the daguerreotype and the calotype, gained widespread acceptance. Of these, the calotype is most closely related to modern photographic processes because, unlike the daguerreotype, it utilized a negative from which a number of positive prints could be made.

The primary responsibility for the invention of the calotype lies with William Henry Fox Talbot. Born in 1800 in Dorset, England, Talbot was a quintessential nineteenth century gentleman who applied his considerable intellect to a broad range of subjects and had great faith in the powers of reason and observation. He graduated with a degree in mathematics from Cambridge University in 1821, and, by the time he had reached his mid-thirties, had published translations of Assyrian texts, several papers on mathematics, a book of prose and poetry, and had been the recipient of several major scientific honors. He had also been elected to the House of Commons and the Royal Society. His interest in developing a ''photographic'' process began during a vacation in Italy in 1833. Such a trip was an almost obligatory ritual for an Englishman of his class. As part of this ritual, Talbot attempted to sketch scenes from the area around Lake Como with the aid of a camera obscura and a camera lucida, the latter an apparatus which used a prism to assist an artist in tracing a view. Talbot was not trained as an artist, and he realized that his drawings would always be clumsy and inadequate, even with the aid of such devices. Pondering the ephemeral image cast onto the ground glass of the camera obscura, he thought "how charming it would be if it were possible to cause these natural images to imprint themselves durably, and remain fixed upon the paper."[1] Thus the desire which originally motivated Talbot to invent a photographic process corresponds closely to that of a modern tourist who, as part of a social ritual, uses the holiday snapshot as a method of appropriating the pastoral or exotic.

Upon his return to England, Talbot, who was aware that certain silver-salt compounds were sensitive to light, began research into a process which would allow nature to reproduce itself "by the agency of Light alone, without any aid whatever from the artist's pencil."[2] By 1834 he was able to sensitize paper using a silver nitrate and sodium chloride solution, and to produce an image by placing objects such as leaves or pieces of lace in contact with the sensitized paper and then exposing it directly to light. No camera was involved in this process. The result was a dark ground with the outline and some internal detail of the object in lighter tones. These images were not permanent and would darken very quickly if exposed to a strong light source; even if kept in a dark place such as a drawer, they would eventually disappear. Talbot learned to stabilize these "photogenic drawings" using a salt solution which reduced the light sensitivity of the silver compound. He believed that this process made the image permanent, an assumption which later proved to be incorrect. Nonetheless, the photogenic drawings were stable enough to be exposed to light for extended periods of time, and it was possible to use the original as a negative to produce positive images in which the tones would be reversed (the terms negative and positive were not used by Talbot until they were later suggested to him by Sir John Herschel).

Early in 1835 Talbot learned to make the paper more sensitive to light by applying alternate solutions of silver nitrate and salt. The increased sensitivity allowed him to expose the paper in a solar microscope and, later, in a small camera obscura which he had constructed himself. The earliest existing image produced using this process in a camera obscura is of a latticed window in Talbot's residence, Lacock Abbey, and was made in August of 1835. Although his process was at a very primitive stage and required a great deal of refinement before it could have any practical application, Talbot devoted little time to further research until early in 1839.

On January 7 of that year, the scientist François Arago announced to the French Academy of Sciences that Louis Daguerre, a Parisian artist and entrepreneur, had discovered a process which would permanently fix the image formed in a camera obscura. Daguerre, with Arago's assistance, proposed that the French government purchase the rights to his process and publish the procedures so that, in France at least, anyone could use the process without paying Daguerre a royalty. Talbot quickly learned of the announcement. Fearing, incorrectly, that Daguerre's process was similar to his own, he hastened to publish his experiments and to refine further his process. He also wrote to the French Academy claiming priority for aspects of Daguerre's process and presented a paper entitled "Some Account of the Art of Photogenic Drawing; or the Processes by which Natural Objects may be used to delineate themselves without the aid of the Artist's pencil" to the Royal Society in London on January 31, 1839. Accounts of that meeting and summations of Talbot's paper, which mention the results of his experiments but no details of the means by which they were obtained, were published in the English press.

In the following months it became apparent that the processes were quite different. While Talbot's process used paper as a support, Daguerre's used a silver-plated sheet of copper. The silver was polished to a mirrorlike surface and exposed to iodine vapors which combined with the silver to form silver iodide. The plate was then exposed in a camera obscura. Following the exposure, it was placed over a container of hot mercury. The mercury vapors condensed on the plate and formed a whitish compound in the areas which had been struck by light. The resulting image would appear either positive or negative, depending upon the angle from which the plate was viewed. The daguerreotype would carry very precise detail and an extremely subtle range of tones. Each was unique and could not be reproduced. The polished silver surface gave it a jewel-like quality, and the daguerreotype often assumed the status of a precious fetishistic object. During the 1840s and early 1850s, families often had daguerreotypes made of a child after its death, as if the image could magically preserve some aspect of the child's soul.

The originality of each process and possible applications of photography were the subject of debate by English and French academicians. Arago's report on the daguerreotype to the French Chamber of Deputies summarizes some of the potential uses of the medium:

> . . . everyone will imagine the extraordinary advantages which could have been derived from so exact and rapid a means of reproduction during the expedition to Egypt; everybody will realize that had we had photography in 1798 we would possess today faithful pictorial records of that which the learned world is forever deprived of by the greed of the Arabs and the vandalism of certain travelers.

> To copy the millions of hieroglyphics which cover even the exterior of the great monuments of Thebes, Memphis, Karnak and others would require decades of time and legions of draughtsmen. By daguerreotype one person would suffice to accomplish this immense work successfully.[3]

Arago also quoted the painter Delaroche who declared that daguerreotypes were

> so far reaching in the realization of certain essential requirements of art that they will be the subject of observation and study, even by the most able painters . . . the painter finds in this process an easy way of making collections for afterstudy.[4]

Photography, then, was seen as an applied art which would be used as an aid to science or to art rather than as a medium on the same aesthetic plane as painting.

In August of 1839, the French government, on Arago's recommendation, purchased the rights to the daguerreotype by providing Daguerre and Isidore Niepce, the son of Daguerre's late partner, with substantial pensions. The government then "donated" the process to the world at large, allowing daguerreotypes to be made without the payment of license fees. The exception to this arrangement was England where, it seems for no reason other than spite, practitioners would be required to purchase a license.

Although Talbot's achievements were recognized by the Royal Society, he received no government support or financial compensation and was bitter at the relative lack of recognition.[5] Daguerre had announced his process first, and he received the bulk of public acclaim.

The announcement of the daguerreotype had prompted Talbot to make several improvements to his own process during the early months of 1839. Most importantly he began, upon the suggestion of Sir John Herschel, to fix his images with "hypo" (sodium thiosulfate). Unlike the salt solutions which Talbot had used previously, hypo fixed the image permanently by removing the unexposed silver-salt compounds from the paper support. Talbot also began to wax his paper negatives in order to make them more translucent and to counteract the effect of the paper fibers which diffused light and reduced the sharpness of the positive print.

The image in Talbot's photogenic drawings would appear spontaneously during exposure, gradually building in density until the exposure was ended. This commonly took thirty minutes or longer. To produce a positive print, the negative was placed on top of a sheet of sensitized paper; both were placed in a wooden printing frame and exposed to sunlight. The image would gradually form on the sensitized paper. Once it had reached the desired density, the paper was removed from the frame in subdued light and fixed. In September of 1840 Talbot accidentally stumbled upon his most important discovery — that the latent or invisible image formed during a relatively short exposure of paper sensitized with potassium iodide, silver nitrate and gallic acid could be "developed" or intensified using a solution of silver nitrate and gallic acid. This method yielded more predictable results and allowed Talbot to reduce his exposure to as little as thirty seconds in bright sunlight. The new process was used to obtain the negative only. The print, later referred to as a salted paper print, was obtained in the same manner as the positive photogenic drawings.

Talbot called this process the calotype after the Greek *kalos* meaning beautiful or that which is good or useful, and *typos* meaning impression. On February 8, 1841, he applied for a patent and in June of that year made public the details of his process, which also came to be known as the talbotype. The result of Talbot's securing a patent was that calotypists in England, Wales, France and the U.S.A. were required to purchase licenses until 1851, when he relinquished patent control of the calotype for all purposes except professional portraiture.

Although it never achieved the immense popularity of the daguerreotype,[6] the calotype eventually was widely used throughout Europe, especially after the Frenchman, Louis Desiré Blanquart-Evrard, published details of an improved version of the calotype process (without mentioning Talbot) in 1847. While the daguerreotype could hold finer detail and a longer and more subtle range of tones, the calotype had several advantages. The most important was that a number of prints could be produced from a single negative. In addition, the materials required to make a calotype were more economical, and the process simpler to perform. It was also safer, as at least one step of the daguerreotype process was potentially lethal.

During the winter of 1843-44, Talbot set up a commercial calotype printing establishment in Reading. Eventually, similar businesses were established on the continent, and manufacturers started to make paper specifically for photographic use. In the summer of 1844 Talbot began to publish *The Pencil of Nature*, the first book to be illustrated with photographs. It included twenty-four tipped-in salted paper prints, as well as descriptions of the calotype process and its possible applications.

During the late 1850s, the calotype and daguerreotype were gradually replaced by the wet-collodion process which used glass, rather than paper, as a support for the negative. Wet-collodion photographs combined the sharpness of the daguerreotype with the possibility of making multiple prints. By 1860 the daguerreotype and the calotype were no longer in common use.

The calotype was introduced to Scotland by Talbot's friend, Sir David Brewster (cat. 5), who, together with Major Lyon Playfair and Dr. John Adamson, Robert Adamson's older brother, experimented with the process in early 1841. Robert Adamson learned of the process from his brother. The younger Adamson had intended to take up a career as an engineer, but, his health not

Cat. 5 *Sir David Brewster*

being up to such physically demanding work, he decided to make his living as a photographer. In May of 1843, Robert Adamson set up Edinburgh's first calotype studio in Rock House on Calton Hill. This location was well suited to his purposes for the garden of the house faced south and received direct sunlight yet was sheltered from the wind by the surrounding stone walls. Talbot's patent did not apply in Scotland, and Adamson was not required to pay a license fee.

The commonly held view of the motive which led to the formation, in July of 1843, of the partnership between Adamson and David Octavius Hill, is that Hill wished to make photographic portraits of the founders of the Free Church of Scotland to be used as reference material for a monumental history painting of the signing of the Act of Separation from the established church. When Sir David Brewster heard that Hill intended to paint such a picture, which would include portraits of up to five hundred individuals, he suggested that the new medium of photography would provide a quick and accurate method of securing a likeness of each of the Free Church's founders before they dispersed to their presbyteries.

Cat. 74 *Sophia Finlay and Harriet Farnie*

Contemporary newspaper accounts and letters from Brewster to Talbot indicate that, while the possibility of making the portrait studies brought about the initial contact, the formal partnership was in fact formed out of an interest in the commercial graphic potential of the calotype, such as the production of prints for book illustrations.[7] Given this kind of application, the possibility of producing a number of prints from a single negative would have been particularly important.

The traditional view of the roles in the partnership is that Hill was responsible for the composition and structure of the images, while Adamson acted primarily as technician. A number of points can be cited in support of this position. Unlike Hill, Adamson had no formal training in art and would not have been familiar with the tradition of academic painting with which much of their work is aligned. Hill stated in his correspondence that his ''. . . connection with the art has been purely that of an artist. I know not the process though it is done under my nose continually and I believe I never will.''[8] The works which were included in the exhibitions of the Royal Scottish Academy between 1844 and 1846 were credited to Robert Adamson under the artistic direction of D.O. Hill. However, this view of the partnership would seem to be oversimplified. Sara Stevenson has pointed out that both partners were often absent from Rock House for extended periods of time, either due to illness or business elsewhere, and both Adamson and Hill would sometimes have been on their own.[9] Adamson also had assistants who handled some aspects of the process. After Adamson's death in

1848, Hill maintained an interest in photography but was unable to find a satisfactory working partner, which suggests that Adamson's role was more than purely technical. Substantial documentation on Hill has survived while very little is known of Adamson, a situation which emphasizes Hill's perceived dominance of the partnership. It is quite possible that their respective roles have been a little too rigidly delineated, perhaps to fit the conception that "artistic genius" must be separated from technical skill.

In addition to the possibility of producing multiple prints, Hill and Adamson's interest in the calotype had an aesthetic basis. As James Borcoman has pointed out, the calotype was well suited for use by artists trained in the concept of "pictorial effect."[10] In early nineteenth century Europe, most academic painters, such as D.O. Hill, based their compositions on expressively arranged masses of light and dark, and emphasized form over sharply defined detail. This methodology could not easily be adapted to the daguerreotype. That process, within the range of focus, reproduced everything in fine detail, giving equal emphasis to trivial and important elements. The daguerreotype image seemed to float in front of the mirrorlike surface of the plate, unlike the calotype in which the image seemed to be impregnated in the paper surface in the manner of an etching or lithograph. Hill had had daguerreotype portraits made prior to the establishment of the partnership and found the process unsatisfactory. He commented that

> the rough surface, and unequal texture throughout the paper is the main cause of the Calotype failing in details, before the process of Daguerreotypy — and this is the very life of it. They [calotypes] look like the imperfect work of man and not the much diminished perfect work of God.[11]

In addition to its lack of sharpness, the calotype's limited tonal range was suited to the concept of pictorial effect. The process could not hold detail in the shadows and highlights at the same time. When highlight detail was emphasized, the shadows would function primarily as shape, and information in these areas would be suppressed. The important elements of the image then could be emphasized through careful consideration of the lighting. Hill and Adamson were able to manipulate light by using reflectors such as a concave mirror or scrims made from light-colored fabric on wooden stretchers.

The process which Adamson used was basically the same as Talbot's, although he made some refinements.[12] Salt prints made at this time could have a range of tones from yellowish sepia to purple, due to a number of variables in the process. Many of Hill and Adamson's prints can be identified by a unqiue reddish-brown tone which is very rich and quite different from the purplish or sepia tones of other salt prints (cat. 74 and others). In comparison

Cat. 120 *Mons Meg*

Cat. 4 *John Blackie*

to the work of other calotypists, Hill and Adamson's prints have particularly subtle gradations and a long tonal range. This is partly due to the hazy atmosphere of nineteenth century Edinburgh, which provided a very diffuse light.

As can be seen from the examples included in this exhibition (cats. 113, 121, 122, 123), the calotype negatives were sometimes retouched with pencil or ink wash. This was done for several reasons. Impurities in the paper support or uneven application of the sensitizing solutions could cause mottling or blotches in the image. Skies, in particular, were considered to be a problem. Like most early photographic processes, the calotype was sensitive only to blue light, and an exposure which was long enough to record detail in landscape or architecture would result in a washed-out sky. Imperfections were especially visible in the lighter areas of the image, and could combine with partially formed cloud details to form an odd mottling. This is evident in the image of Mons Meg (cat. 120); the imperfections are in the negative, not the modern salt print. While the resulting spatial ambiguity may seem interesting to a viewer today, Hill and Adamson considered it distracting and would remove it by drawing on the negative.

Because exposures would regularly last thirty seconds or longer, Hill and Adamson often used supports, headrests or tripods to steady their subjects. Negatives were retouched, sometimes quite crudely, to remove these from the final print. Evidence of this can be seen in *Mrs. Logan, Mrs. Seton and two unknown men* (negative cat. 113, positive cat. 112), *Unknown Women* (cat. 115), as well as other images in the exhibition.

Retouching was also done to emphasize detail which had been lost because of movement during the exposure or simply because the medium could not record some fine detail which the artists considered important. In *John Blackie* (cat. 4), Hill's name, which appears on the spine of one of the books, has been drawn on the negative. In *Rev. Hugh MacKay MacKenzie* (cat. 26), the print on the cover of the book which the subject is holding has been drawn on the negative. The image has also been reversed, from left to right, in comparison to other prints from the same negative. The negatives for images of George Cook (cat. 9) and Abraham Capadose (cats. 7, 8) have been retouched in order to accentuate the forehead, hairline or other facial details. Hill and Adamson often emphasized the forehead (and thus the intellectual capacity) of the male academics, but rarely the women or working-class men among their subjects. Occasionally the print itself has been touched up, although possibly by someone other than Hill and Adamson, as in *Jeanie Wilson* (cat. 101).

David Octavius Hill and Robert Adamson, and other early photographers who situated their work in a fine art context, did not make a radical break with earlier modes of representation. As may be seen from this discussion, the calotype process they chose to work with allowed them to combine photographic qualities, such as perceived objectivity, with the opportunity to idealize the image and align it with existing pictorial traditions.

Cat. 9 *Rev. Dr. George Cook*

NOTES

1. Talbot, W.H.F. *The Pencil of Nature.* London: Longman, Brown, Green & Longmans, 1844-46. Reprint, with introduction by Beaumont Newhall, New York: Da Capo Press, 1969. unpaginated.

2. ibid.

3. Arago, François. "Report." Quoted in J.M. Eder's *History of Photography,* translated by Edward Epsteam. (New York: Columbia University Press, 1945. Reprinted New York: Dover Publications, 1978): 234. For a discussion of the ideology of Arago's position and some of the broader social implications of photography in general, see Allan Sekula's essay "The Traffic in Photographs," in *Photography Against The Grain: Essays and Photo Works 1973-1983.* Halifax: The Press of the Nova Scotia College of Art and Design, 1984.

4. ibid. p. 235

5. Talbot fared better than Hippolyte Bayard, a Frenchman who invented his own paper-based process. As Bayard did not have the same access to the scientific community as Daguerre or Talbot, he received almost no recognition at all.

6. In the city of Paris during 1846, two thousand daguerreotype cameras and five hundred thousand daguerreotype plates were sold. By 1850, there were two thousand daguerreotypists working in the United States. It is estimated that between 1840 and 1860 thirty million photographs, a large percentage of them daguerreotypes, were made in the United States. Source: *Photography and Society* by Gisele Freund. (Boston: David R. Godine Inc., 1980): 30, 33.

7. See Ralph L. Harley Jr.'s "The Partnership Motive of D.O. Hill and Robert Adamson" published in *History of Photography* vol. 10, no. 4, Oct.-Dec. 1986, pp. 303-312.

8. Letter from D.O. Hill to David Roberts, 12 March 1845. Quoted in Sara Stevenson's essay "Robert Adamson and David Octavius Hill" in the exhibition catalogue *Printed Light.* (Edinburgh: Scottish National Portrait Gallery and HMSO, 1986): 33.

9. ibid. pp. 32-33.

10. See James Borcoman's essay in the exhibition catalogue *The Painter as Photographer.* Ottawa: The National Gallery of Canada, 1978, unpaginated.

11. Letter from D.O. Hill to Mr. Bicknell, 17 January 1848. Quoted in *The History of Photography* by Beaumont Newhall. (New York: The Museum of Modern Art, 1964): 37.

12. In a letter to David Roberts, 14 March 1845, Hill states: "I believe Dr. Adamson and his brother to be the fathers of many of these parts of the process which make it a valuable and practical art. I believe also from all I have seen that Robert Adamson is the most successful manipulator the art has yet seen, and his steady industry and knowledge of chemistry, is such that both from him and his brother much new improvements may yet be expected." This letter is quoted in Sara Stevenson's essay in *Printed Light,* pp. 36-38.

Catalogue Of The Exhibition

Entries By Keith Bell And David Harris

Frequently cited references are:
Stevenson, Sara, *David Octavius Hill and Robert Adamson, Catalogue of Their Calotypes Taken Between 1843 and 1847 in the Collection of the Scottish National Portrait Gallery.* Edinburgh: National Galleries of Scotland, 1981.

and

Ward, John, and Sara Stevenson. *Printed Light, The Scientific Art of William Henry Fox Talbot and David Octavius Hill with Robert Adamson.* Edinburgh: Scottish National Portrait Gallery, and Her Majesty's Stationery Office, 1986.

Abbreviations: GUL, Glasgow University Library; SNPG, Scottish National Portrait Gallery

Print Sizes are as follows:
Size 1, 43.0 × 32.6 cm
Size 2, 29.9 × 26.7 cm
Size 3, 29.9 × 22.8 cm
Size 4, 20.8 × 15.7 cm
Size 5, 15.6 × 11.5 cm

Portraits

1. Rev. Thomas Bain
GUL 13. Size 4
Bain (1815-1884) was the Free Church Minister at Mortlach and Coupar Angus. K.B.

2. John Maclaren Barclay
GUL 14. Size 4
Barclay (1811-1886) was a portrait painter and member of the Royal Scottish Academy. K.B.

3. Rev. Thomas Blizzard Bell
GUL 18. Size 4. Reproduced front cover
Bell (1815-1886) was a Free Church minister. This calotype was used for the Disruption picture (cat. 41). K.B.

4. John Blackie
GUL 21. Size 4. Reproduced p. 46
Blackie (1805-1873), a publisher, is leaning on two books: *The Land of Burns*, illustrated by Hill and with the photographer's name added to the spine on the negative (GUL collection), and Turner's *Liber Studiorum.* K.B.

5. Sir David Brewster
GUL 23. Size 4. Reproduced p. 43
Brewster (1781-1868) was a physicist, calotypist, principal of United College, St. Andrews, and vice-chancellor of Edinburgh University. He was instrumental in introducing the calotype to Scotland through his correspondence with Fox Talbot whose calotype process was patented in England in 1841. Working at St. Andrews with Major Playfair and Dr. John Adamson, Brewster experimented with the process. During 1843, he was also instrumental in persuading Dr. John Adamson's younger brother, Robert, to set up as a professional photographer in Edinburgh, following Fox Talbot's wish that the calotype process should be established in Scotland in a professional manner. In June 1843, Brewster suggested to D.O. Hill that he might use calotype portraits as studies for his projected painting of the Disruption. (cat. 41).

Despite this initial enthusiasm, Brewster was not entirely satisfied with the use of calotype in portraiture. "I have been very much struck," he told Fox Talbot in 1843, "with the *different* calotypes of the *same person.* In many of them, where the sitter was steady, the family likeness is scarcely preserved. Compare the enclosed one of myself with those taken by you. Does this arise from the camera? I have seen among Mr. Adamson's calotypes pictures of men and women in one of which the sitter was decidedly good looking and in the other hideous." (Science Museum, London, ms. letter of 28 November 1843, quoted by Stevenson in *Printed Light,* p. 125). K.B.

6. Archibald Butter of Faskally
GUL 42. Size 4

7. Rev. Dr. Abraham Capadose
SNPG, a. Size 4

8. Rev. Dr. Abraham Capadose
GUL 49. Size 4

9. Rev. Dr. George Cook
GUL 57. Size 4. Reproduced p. 47

10. Donaldson
GUL 72. Size 4

11. Charles Drysdale
GUL 76. Size 4

12. Rev. Dr. Henry Duncan
GUL 79. Size 4
Duncan (1774-1846) was moderator of the
General Assembly of the Free Church of
Scotland in 1836. K.B.

13. Thomas Duncan
GUL 83. Size 4
Duncan (1807-1845) was a Scottish portrait,
genre and history painter. K.B.

14. William Etty
SNPG, a. Size 4. Reproduced p. 28
Etty (1787-1849), an artist, visited Edinburgh on
16 and 17 October 1844. While on the visit, he
was entertained at a banquet by members of the
Royal Scottish Academy, delivered an address to
the students and, with his brother Walter,
established two prizes for original design. The
negative of SNPG,c is inscribed ''Mr. Etty Octo
16-44,'' which suggests a probable date for the
present work as well (Stevenson, p.59). K.B.

15. John Hope Finlay
SNPG, a. Size 4
John Hope Finlay (1839-1907) was the son of
Charles Finlay, a solicitor and keeper of the
General Register of Sasines of Scotland
(Stevenson, p.61). K.B.

16. George Gordon
GUL 104. Size 4
Gordon was the writing master at Madras
College, St. Andrews. All Hill and Adamson's
calotypes show him in the active practise of his
profession (SNPG a-d). One negative for SNPG d,
is inscribed ''Mr. Gordon Aug. 24 44 DF Last
Gum [or Sun],'' which suggests a probable date
for the present work. This is a variant. K.B.

17. James Greig
GUL 107. Size 4

18. George Gunn
GUL 111. Size 4
Gunn was a factor to the Duke of Sutherland. K.B.

19. Robert Horsburgh
GUL. 135. Size 4

20. Rev. Peter Jones
SNPG, a. Size 4
Jones (1802-1856), or Kahkewaquonaby meaning
''sacred feathers'' in Ojibwa, was a Mississauga
Ojibwa chief, member of the eagle totem,
farmer, Methodist minister, author and
translator. He was born on Burlington Heights in
1802, the second son of Augustus Jones, a
surveyor and Sarah Henry, daughter of a
Mississauga chief. In 1823, he became a
Methodist convert and in 1829 he was made a
chief of the Credit band. Together with his
brother John, Peter Jones prepared the earliest
translations of the Bible into Ojibwa.

In 1831, 1837 and 1845, Jones toured Britain
to raise money for his missionary work among
the Indians. It was on his third visit in 1845 that
he posed for Hill and Adamson's camera. Jones
was received by large crowds in Scotland but
found the continual travelling depressing. In a
letter of 23 October to his wife, Eliza, he
commented: ''I am getting heartily tired of
begging,'' and complained that the British only
wanted to see him as an exotic object dressed in
his ''odious'' native costume. Jones made one
hundred and fifty addresses wearing Indian
costume during his 1831 tour of Britain; both he
and his wife believed that Christian and
European society represented the highest level
of human existence. Despite these objections,
Jones posed in native costume in at least four
Hill and Adamson calotypes in which he was
arranged in a ''natural'' setting in the garden of
Rock House. In five other calotypes, however,
Jones appeared in western clothing, perhaps at
his own insistence K.B.

21. Rev. Peter Jones
SNPG,a, calotype negative for cat. 20. Size 4

22. Rev. Alexander Keith
GUL 150. Size 4
Keith (1791-1880) was the Free Church Minister
of St. Cyrus, as well as a writer on prophecy
(Stevenson, p. 76). K.B.

23. George Meikle Kemp
GUL 152. Size 4
Kemp (1795-1844) was the architect for the
Scott Monument where he was photographed by
Hill and Adamson. K.B.

24. Lane
GUL 157. Size 4
The subject of this portrait has been called
"John Lane," "Dr. Lane" and "Edward William
Lane" (cat. 79). K.B.

25. Robert Lindley, Yorkshire Cellist
GUL 410. Size 4
Lindley was a professor at the Royal Academy of
Music. K.B.

26. Rev. Hugh MacKay MacKenzie
GUL 178. Size 4

27. John Ban Mackenzie
GUL LSP. Size 4. Reproduced p. 32
Mackenzie (1796-1858) was piper to the Marquis
of Breadalbane and the Highland Society.
Portraits of men in Highland dress (including
clan pipers) were common in Scottish painting
(e.g., Raeburn's *Colonel Alasdair Mcdonnell of
Glengarry*, 1812, coll. National Galleries of
Scotland). Hill used a standing portrait of
Mackenzie as a study for his painting *Edinburgh
from the Castle, 1847* (coll. National Galleries of
Scotland). K.B.

28. Rev. Angus Mackintosh McGillivray
GUL 176. Size 4

29. Hugh Miller
GUL LSP. Size 2
Miller (1802-1856) began his working life as a
stonemason. He educated himself as a geologist
and made a number of important discoveries. He
also had a career as a journalist during which
he edited *The Witness* from 1839 to 1856. Hill
and Adamson made several calotype studies of
him, two as a stonemason in Calton cemetery
(SNPG a,b) and another which was used for the
Disruption picture. K.B.

30. Professor James Miller
GUL 190. Size 4
Miller (1812-1864) was professor of surgery at
Edinburgh University, as well as an orator and
temperance reformer (Stevenson, p. 91) K.B.

31. Jimmy Miller
GUL 334. Size 4
Jimmy was the son of Professor James Miller. K.B.

32. John Murray
GUL 204. Size 4
Murray, (1808-1892) was the publisher of the
influential *Quarterly Review*, as well as a
number of important books, including
Livingstone's *Travels* (1857), Darwin's *Origin of
the Species* (1859) and Kugler's *History of
Painting*. Lady Eastlake first met D.O. Hill at one
of Murray's Edinburgh dinner parties. K.B.

33. James Nasmyth
SNPG, c. Size 4. Reproduced p. 33
Nasmyth (1808-1890), an engineer and
astronomer, was the inventor of the steam
hammer. He was the son of the painter Patrick
Nasmyth (1787-1831, known as the "English
Hobbema"), and was himself a highly competent
artist, a factor which may have led to his
friendship with D.O. Hill. K.B.

34. Sir Lyon Playfair
GUL 213. Size 4
1st Baron Playfair of St. Andrews (1818-1898). K.B.

35. Patrick, Lord Robertson
GUL 219. Size 4
Lord Robertson (1794-1855) was a judge,
chairman of the Chamber of Advocates, and
in 1848, lord rector of the University of
Aberdeen. K.B.

36. Rev. Samuel Smith
GUL 236. Size 4
Smith was a Free Church minister from Borgue. K.B.

37. Dr. George Smyttan
GUL 239. Size 4

38. *Robert Cunningham Graham Speirs*
GUL 240. Size 4

Speirs (1797-1847) was an advocate, sheriff of Midlothian, leading free churchman and prison reformer (Stevenson, p. 105). K.B.

39. *Sir John Robert Steell*
GUL 242. Size 4

Steell (1804-1891), a sculptor, carved the statue of Sir Walter Scott for the Scott Monument in Edinburgh. K.B.

40. *John Stevens*
SNPG, a. Size 4

John Stevens (c. 1793-1868) was a painter of portrait and subject pictures, and a member of the Royal Scottish Academy. The sculpture, entitled "The Last of the Romans," was made by Stevens. It was also used by Hill in another calotype, *The Morning After "He Greatly Daring Dined"* (SNPG, G134.). K.B.

41. *David Welsh*
GUL 254. Size 5

Welsh was professor of church history at Edinburgh University and professor of divinity at New College, Edinburgh. As moderator of the Assembly of the Church of Scotland in 1843, he read the protest and headed a carefully planned walkout of one hundred and fifty ministers, which led to the formation of a Free Church. This action arose in part over the issue of the increasing power of the owners of presentations of livings, who were able to appoint ministers over the objections of the presbyteries. The Disruption and the subsequent signing of the Act of Separation and Deed of Demission at Tanfield, Edinburgh, in May 1843, attracted the attention of the painter D.O. Hill, who determined to paint a picture of the event. Shortly after Hill advertised his intention (*The Witness* 24 May 1843), Sir David Brewster (cat. 5), who was involved in the Free Church, suggested to Hill

that he might use calotype portraits of the people present at the assembly, as a means of obtaining likenesses for the painting. Brewster subsequently informed Fox Talbot of his actions in a letter of 3 July:

"A grand historical picture is undertaken by a first rate Artist, to represent the *first General Assembly of the Free Church*. I got hold of the artist — showed him the Calotype, and the eminent advantage he might derive from it in getting likenesses of all the principal characters before they were dispersed to their respective homes. He was at first incredulous, but went to Mr. Adamson, and arranged with him the preliminaries for getting all the necessary portraits." (ms. letter, 3 July 1843, coll. Science Museum, quoted by Stevenson, *Printed Light*, p. 156.) K.B.

42. *Unidentified Portrait* (Cpt. Martin?)
GUL 188. Size 4

43. *Unknown Man* (Maxwell Gunn?)
GUL 112. Size 4

44. *Unknown Man*
GUL 266. Size 4

45. *Unknown Man*
GUL 272. Size 4

46. *Unknown Man*
GUL 283. Size 4

47. *Madame d'Aubigne*
SNPG, a. Size 4

48. *Miss Crampton*
SNPG, a. Size 4. Reproduced p. 32

Miss Crampton is posed like a fashion plate, wearing a striped silk dress and carrying a fashionable small parasol. Her bonnet and tartan wrap are displayed on either side on a chair and table. K.B.

49. Mrs. Mary (Gray) Duncan
GUL 303. Size 4
Mrs. Duncan was the widow of Rev. Robert Lundie and wife of Rev. Henry Duncan. K.B.

50. Lady Elizabeth (Rigby) Eastlake
GUL 307. Size 4
An essayist and critic, Elizabeth Rigby (1809-1893) began her writing career with an essay on Göethe for the *Foreign Quarterly Review* in 1836. This was followed by a book, *Letters from the Shores of the Baltic* (1841), published by John Murray. Through her connection with Murray, she began to write regularly for the *Quarterly Review* (1842-) on a wide variety of subjects including ''Lady Travellers,'' ''German Painting,'' a notorious attack on Austen's *Jane Eyre*, and an important early essay on photography in 1857 (Vol. CI, pp. 442-468). She met Hill and Adamson after her family moved to Edinburgh in 1842. In 1849 she married Sir Charles Lock Eastlake (1793-1865), an artist, future president of the Royal Academy of Arts, and president of the Royal Photographic Society, at which time she moved to 7 Fitzroy Square, London. There she continued her literary production, finishing Anna Jameson's *History of Our Lord in Works of Art* after Jameson's death and writing for the *Quarterly*. Hill made at least sixteen different calotypes of Elizabeth Rigby (SNPG a-p), as well as including her in several groups (SNPG, G221-225). K.B.

51. Lady Elizabeth (Rigby) Eastlake
SNPG, g. Size 4

52. Lady Elizabeth (Rigby) Eastlake
SNPG, j. Size 5. Reproduced p. 22
Several of Hill and Adamson's calotypes of Eastlake suggest a subject picture rather than a simple portrait. As Stevenson (*Printed Light*, p. 128) has suggested, these works — including the present one — suggest a Spanish or Italian sentimental theme, hence the shawl draped over her head. K.B.

53. Mrs. Anna (Brownell Murphy) Jameson
SNPG, a. Size 4
Mrs. Jameson (1794-1860) was an art historian and essayist who established her reputation with the publication of *The Diary of an Ennuyée* in 1826. Subsequently, after a short stay in Canada where her husband, Robert Jameson, was a judge, she published *Winter Studies and Summer Rambles in Canada* (1838). This was followed by a number of books on art including *Memoirs of the Early Italian Painters* (1845); four volumes of *Sacred and Legendary Art* (1848-52), the last of which was completed after her death by Lady Eastlake; and in 1854 *A Commonplace Book of Thoughts, Memories and Fancies, original and selected*. K.B.

54. Mrs. Kinloch
SNPG, a. Size 4. Reproduced p. 32

55. Miss Lockhart
GUL 345. Size 4
Hill and Adamson posed Miss Lockhart in at least four different ways. This work is the most relaxed (SNPG, a-d). K.B.

56. Miss Elizabeth Logan
GUL 331. Size 4
Miss Logan was the daughter of Alexander Stuart Logan. The theme of ''Sleep'' or ''The Age of Innocence'' was a popular one in nineteenth century art. Hill photographed ''sleeping'' children, including his own daughter Charlotte (*Printed Light*, p. 139), on a number of occasions. Small children were easier to photograph ''asleep'' when movement during the long exposure was less likely. This is evident in Hill's attempts (SNPG, e, f) to photograph Elizabeth Logan while she was awake. K.B.

57. Miss McCandlish
GUL 316. Size 4

58. Miss Patricia Morris
GUL 317. Size 4
Morris is posed like a figure in a Victorian sentimental painting. K.B.

59. Miss Justine Monro (Mrs. Gallie)
GUL 309. Size 4

60. Miss Murray
GUL 320. Size 4
Miss Murray was the sister of John Murray, the publisher. K.B.

61. Mrs. Anne (Palgrave) Rigby
GUL 321. Size 4
Mrs. Rigby (1777-1872) was the mother of Lady Elizabeth Eastlake and Mrs. Matilda Smith (cats. 50 and 62). Like her daughter Elizabeth, Mrs. Rigby was a frequent subject for Hill and Adamson's camera (SNPG, a-l). K.B.

62. Mrs. Matilda (Rigby) Smith
SNPG, a. Size 4
Mrs. Smith was the daughter of Mrs. Anne (Palgrave) Rigby (cat. 61). With a few exceptions (notably *Mrs. Isabella (Burns) Begg*, SNPG, a), Hill's female subjects do not look directly at the camera. In this case, Mrs. Smith posed in an alert, attentive manner, without the more usual self-conscious arrangement of head and hands which recalls contemporary fashion plates and book illustrations. K.B.

---

63. Unknown Woman
GUL 325. Size 4

---

65. Dr. George Bell, Miss Bell and Rev. Thomas Bell
GUL 337. Size 4
George Bell was one of the founders of "ragged schools," a commissioner in lunacy and a friend of D.O. Hill (Stevenson p. 41). Thomas Blizzard Bell (1815-1886) was a Free Church minister. Miss Bell later became Lady Moncrieff. K.B.

---

66. Misses Binney and Mrs. Justine Gallie
SNPG, G37. Size 4

64. The Adamson Family
GUL 336. Size 4
The persons in this portrait are Dr. John Adamson, unknown woman, (perhaps Mrs. Alexander Adamson), Alexander Adamson, Miss Melville Adamson and Robert Adamson. Dr. John Adamson was the first man to take a calotype portrait in Scotland. His brother Robert, D.O. Hill's partner, improved the process and achieved a high level of quality and consistency in calotype production. K.B.

---

67. Misses Binney
GUL 339. Size 4
This combination of sisterhood and romantic reverie was probably intended as a reflection upon the end of companionable childhood and the possibilities of future love and marriage. The subject had been treated in a similar manner a few years before by Sir Charles Eastlake in a painting called *The Two Sisters*, exhibited at the Royal Academy in 1842 (whereabouts unknown, a replica, signed and dated 1844 is in the Royal Collection, Osborne House). K.B.

68. Rev. Dr. Thomas Chalmers and Thomas Chalmers Hanna
GUL 342. Size 2
Thomas Chalmers was a theologian, Free Church leader, first moderator of the Free Church Assembly and principal of New College, Edinburgh. As a minister of the church, he was the leader of a campaign to "rescue" the working classes from what he termed "home heathenism" in Glasgow and Edinburgh. Hill made a number of portraits related to the Disruption picture (SNPG a-h, PG 12-14), as well as with his family at Merchiston Castle (SNPG, G63-66). The present work, taken with a large camera in the garden of the castle, later provided the basis for one of Hill's paintings — *Rev. Dr. Thomas Chalmers and His Grandson* (coll. SNPG). As Stevenson (*Printed Light*, pp. 162-163) has explained, the painting was an allegory of life and death, youth and old age. The theme later became a popular one among photographers including W. Collie and F. Horne. K.B.

69. The Chalmers Family at Merchiston
Later print
GUL LSP. Size 3
Hill and Adamson took a number of photographs of the Chalmers family in the grounds of Merchiston Castle in 1844. K.B.

70. Group at Bonaly Towers
GUL LSP. Size 4
From left to right: John Henning, unknown man, boy and woman (perhaps Mrs. Horner, perhaps Lady Lyell) D.O. Hill, Miss and Mrs. Cockburn, Mrs. Cleghorn and another woman on the stairs and Lord Cockburn (Stevenson, p. 160). Bonaly Towers was the residence of Lord Cockburn, the solicitor-general for Scotland, and the venue for meetings of the Bonaly Friday Club (see *History and Laws of the Bonaly Friday Club*, Edinburgh, 1842). No longer confined by the narrow space in front of Rock House, Hill was able to arrange his subjects against the broader background of the landscape and castle. K.B.

71. Charles and George Drysdale
SNPG, G85. Size 4

72. Miss Wilhelmina Fillans, Miss Fillans and James Fillans
SNPG, G97. Size 4

73. Arthur, John Hope and Sophia Finlay known as "The Minnow Pool"
SNPG, G99. Size 4

74. Sophia Finlay and Harriet Farnie
SNPG, G101. Size 4. Reproduced p. 44
Images of sleeping children reflect popular taste for such sentimental scenes. The presence of the puppy adds to the atmosphere. Lady Eastlake's 1845 reaction to an animal painting by Landseer graphically demonstrates prevailing attitudes: "To the Exhibition [at the Royal Scottish Academy]. Two little Landseers . . . a dog's sorrow is more affecting than a human being's, more grief and less hope; that dog on the field of Austerlitz wrings one's heart." (*Journals and Correspondence of Lady Eastlake ed. by her nephew Charles Eastlake Smith*. London: 1895, p. 159). K.B.

75. John Henning, Alexander Handyside Ritchie and D.O. Hill
GUL 353. Size 4
Henning (1771-1851) began his career as a carpenter and cabinetmaker before turning to sculpture after a visit to Raeburn's studio in Edinburgh in 1799. His production included numerous portrait medallions, as well as casts of the Parthenon and Bassae friezes. Ritchie (1804-1870) was also a sculptor and had worked with Thorwaldson in Rome 1826-29. He returned to Edinburgh in 1830 and made numerous portrait busts in Edinburgh, Stirling, Musselburgh and Glasgow. This group photograph shows the three artists studying a reduced-size copy made by Henning from the Elgin Marbles. K.B.

76. Mrs. Cleghorn and John Henning as Miss Wardour and Edie Ochiltree from Sir Walter Scott's "The Antiquary"
GUL 355. Size 4. Reproduced p. 5
In this tableau made at Lord Cockburn's home Bonaly Towers, Edie Ochiltree, the blue-gowned beggar who has recently rescued Miss Wardour and her father Sir Arthur from a storm on the coast, attempts to convince Miss Wardour of the love borne for her by the young Mr. Lovell (ch. 12 in *The Antiquary*). Ochiltree, a professional beggar known as a King's Bedesman or Blue-gown, wears the "slouched hat of huge dimensions" and the "pewter badge" described earlier in the text (p. 49 in the Constable, *Waverly* edition of 1901). Hill and Adamson may have been planning a series of scenes from Scott's novels. Earlier Hill had provided watercolor studies, which were engraved as illustrations to *The Land of Burns* published by Blackie and Sons, Glasgow, in two volumes in 1840. K.B.

77. D.O. Hill and William Borthwick Johnstone
GUL 360. Size 4
Johnstone, a landscape and history painter, was the first curator of the National Gallery of Scotland. The support which holds Johnstone in place can be seen between the two men. K.B.

**78. William Napier and
Mr. and Mrs. Kinloch**
SNPG, G158. Size 4
Despite the problems created by long exposures,
Hill and Adamson made several successful
calotypes of people shown in apparently
arrested movement — in this case Napier and
the Kinlochs on a "walk." K.B.

80. Masons Working on the Scott Monument
GUL 403. Size 4
This is one of a series of calotypes taken by Hill
and Adamson (SNPG, E12-14) of the masons at
work on the carved ornament for the Scott
Monument, designed by George Meikle Kemp.
While the Portrait Gallery scenes are set against
the dark background of a mason's shed, this print
presents a clean view from the building beside
Princes Street, looking across to the Castle with
the Royal Institution, later the Royal Scottish
Academy, appearing on the right. The conscious
informality of this study is similar to that found
in several of the Newhaven calotypes. K.B.

79. Mr. Lane and Mr. Lewis (?)
GUL 369. Size 4
These two men have sometimes been identified
as Edward William Lane, translator of the
Arabian Nights and John Frederick Lewis,
painter of Middle Eastern subjects. However,
Lane was living in Egypt at the time the Hill
and Adamson partnership was at work and the
identification of Lewis is doubtful. Middle
Eastern subjects by painters such as Wilkie,
Roberts and Eastlake were popular at this time.
(*Printed Light*, p. 150). K.B.

81. Mary and Margaret McCandlish
SNPG, G169. Size 4
As Stevenson has remarked (*Printed Light*,
p. 150), this calotype — with Margaret
McCandlish posing as a milkmaid — is one of
only a few rustic poses arranged by Hill.
Another calotype in this series is known as
"The Gowan" or daisy, perhaps a reference to
Robert Burns' poem "To a Mountain Daisy,"
which is a reverie on the transience and
uncertainty of life (ibid. p. 150). K.B.

82. Agnes and Ellen Milne
GUL 373. Size 4

83. Rev. Moir and John Gibson
SNPG, G195. Size 4
Hill arranged this pair as a conversation piece
with the book as the focus. K.B.

**84. Col. Morison, Robert Cadell,
James Wyld, Alexander Ross**
GUL 374. Size 5
In this unusual composition, Hill used a dark
cloth as a crude backdrop to highlight the men's
heads instead of his more usual props. The
figure of Ross was used for the Disruption
picture. K.B.

**85. Miss Patricia and Miss Isabella Morris
and D.O. Hill**
SNPG, G203. Size 4
Sometimes called "The Sketching Lesson," this
work shows two girls who were friends of the
Hill family. K.B.

**86. Mrs. Anne Rigby and
Lady Elizabeth Eastlake**
GUL 382. Size 4
Mrs. Rigby wears the same damask dress and
old-fashioned double collar in which she appears
in a number of other calotypes. Her daughter is
more fashionably attired in a double-skirted
dress with a shorter, rounded waist, while her
head is framed by the scalloped pattern of the
small parasol. K.B.

**87. Mrs. Mary Watson, Miss Agnes Milne,
Miss Mary Watson, Miss Watson,
Miss Ellen Milne**
Albumen print
SNPG, G259. Size 8.8 × 11.0 cm

88. Baron and Baroness Wharncliffe
GUL 386. Size 4
In their two calotypes of the Wharncliffes,
(cat. 89), Hill and Adamson probably intended
to create the impression of an informal conversation, reversing the position of the two figures
in the present image as a variation. K.B.

89. John Stuart-Wortley, Baron Wharncliffe and Georgina, Baroness Wharncliffe
SNPG, G270. Size 4
John Stuart-Wortley was a member of Parliament and he published several works on the national economy. Georgina Wortley was one of the queens of beauty at the Eglington Tournament. K.B.

90. Presbytery of Auchterarder
GUL 394. Size 4
Rev. Andrew Noble, Rev. James Carment, Rev. John Ferguson, Rev. James Thomson are seated and two unknown men are standing. The figures of Noble, Carment and Thomson were used as studies for the Disruption picture. (Stevenson p. 182). K.B.

NEWHAVEN

91. Newhaven fishwife
GUL 420. Size 4

92. Two English yachtsmen, unknown boy, David Young and unknown man
GUL 424. Size 4
Hill and Adamson usually posed the fishermen and boys on the beach by the village (cat. 109), often using their boats as an appropriate backdrop. The fishing boats and their crews could not be photographed at sea because of the blurring caused by the motion of the boats during the long time exposure. One trial attempt to show a vessel under sail (coll. SNPG) was a simulation, with the craft propped upright on the beach, the crew aboard, and a long pole pushing the sail taut as if in a breeze. However, the composition appears contrived alongside the other, more ''natural'' Newhaven scenes and the experiment was probably not repeated. Later photographers, like George Washington Wilson, took advantage of the faster exposures made possible by the collodion process. They concentrated on fishing boats in the water where the possibilities of reflection and long ocean perspectives could be effectively exploited. K.B.

93. Newhaven houses
GUL 444. Size 4
This view shows the external staircases of the fisherfolks' houses. Various items of equipment, including the ''creels'' used by the women to carry the fish into Edinburgh, may be seen hanging on the stair rails or lying on the ground. K.B.

94. Newhaven houses
SNPG, N65. Size 4

95. Newhaven fishwives
Modern salt print by Michael Gray
GUL 623 (negative). Size 23.6 × 31.5 cm

96. Newhaven fishwives
Modern salt print by Michael Gray
GUL 625 (negative). Size 31.5 × 23.6 cm

97. The pastor's visit (Mrs. Carnie Noble, unknown woman, Bessie Crombie, Mary Combe, Mrs. Margaret (Dryburgh) Lyall, Rev. Dr. James Fairbairn and James Gall)
GUL 442. Size 4
The Rev. Dr. James Fairbairn came to Newhaven in 1838 and seceded with his congregation at the Disruption in 1843. Fairbairn was instrumental in raising money for the modernization of the Newhaven fishing fleet, which had had boats too small for deep sea fishing. Thirty-three large new boats were purchased, each, according to Mrs. Cupples (*Newhaven, its origin and history*, Edinburgh, 1888) costing £250 with a similar amount for fishing gear.

Ford had suggested in *An Early Victorian Album* (New York, 1974, p. 36) that the Newhaven calotypes were taken to support Fairbairn's fund-raising purposes. However, other evidence suggests (see Newhaven essay) that the Hill-Adamson partnership planned a Newhaven album as part of a larger Scottish series. K.B.

98. Two unknown women, Mrs. Margaret (Dryburgh) Lyall, Marion Finlay and Mrs. Grace (Finlay) Ramsay
GUL 434. Size 4

99. Unknown boys
GUL 430. Size 4

100. Unknown children
SNPG, N52. Size 4
Hill and Adamson overcame the difficulties of keeping children still for the long exposure by draping them over an upturned fishing boat, thereby avoiding the awkward poses created by the use of clamps. K.B.

101. Jeanie Wilson
SNPG, N.15. Size 4

102. Unknown boy
SNPG, N8. Size 4
Also called "His faither's breeks" or "King fisher". The boy is shown leaning on a basket of fishing line. K.B.

103. Mrs. Hall
SNPG, N14. Size 4. Reproduced p. 12
This calotype is called "Newhaven Madonna" in the small Hill and Adamson album in the Royal Photographic Society collection, Bath. K.B.

104. Fishergirls
GUL 432. Size 4. Reproduced p. 19
This study is of Mrs. Logan and two unknown women (SNPG, N35) and Hill used it as the basis for a section of his painting of *Edinburgh from the Castle* 1847 (coll. National Galleries of Scotland). The women are shown on the left of the painting, seated on the battlements of Edinburgh Castle. K.B.

105. Mrs. Elizabeth (Johnstone) Hall
GUL 419. Size 4
Hill and Adamson showed their Newhaven subjects not only engaged in work but also in more picturesque poses as illustrated here. Sara Stevenson has remarked (*Printed Light* p. 154) that the bulky and richly patterned dress of the fishwives gave them a flowing sculptural form which contemporaries compared to classical reliefs. For example, Dr. John Brown in a review of the calotypes in 1846 remarked on one portrait of a fishwife: "As easy, as unconfined, as deep-bosomed and ample, as any Greek matron. Indeed we have often been struck, when seeing them sitting together round their oyster creels, with their likeness to those awful and majestic women, the Fates of the Elgin Marbles . . ." (ibid., p. 154). K.B.

**106. The letter (Marion Finlay,
Mrs. Margaret Lyall and Mrs. Grace Ramsay)**
GUL 433. Size 4
As Stevenson pointed out (*Printed Light* p. 155),
the theme of "The Letter" was derived from
seventeenth century Dutch genre paintings and
was intended to introduce added drama to a
scene. Hill posed two women pouring over the
letter, while another, fully loaded with her "creel"
and smaller "scull" (on top), prepares to leave
for the city. The baskets were an integral part of
the women's trade and were included in most of
the calotypes, where they often added a pleasing
shape to the composition. The woman shown
here has her basket strap around her shoulders
instead of across her forehead, the distinctive
manner used by the Newhaven women. A
clamp, partially erased on the negative, may be
seen on the left above the middle woman's
elbow. The photographers often tried to conceal
these by lining them up with joints in the
masonry or against a dark ground. K.B.

107. A Newhaven pilot
SNPG, N6. Size 4
Newhaven provided a large proportion of the
pilots who were certified by Trinity House at
Leith to serve the shipping in the Firth of Forth.
In 1788, twenty-six of the twenty-nine
candidates certified at Leith were from the
village (T. McGowran, *Newhaven-on-Forth. Port
of Grace*, Edinburgh, 1985, p. 42). Pilots were at
the top of the social order in the village and
could earn large fees for helping ships in
difficulties. K.B.

108. Unknown women
SNPG, N50. Size 4
The figures in the Newhaven calotypes were
often posed with a view to creating a relaxed,
informal atmosphere of momentarily arrested
activity. In this, Hill followed the established
practice also found in paintings of scenes of
Scottish life and character by David Allan
(1744-1796), Alexander Carse (-c. 1838), David
Wilkie (1785-1841) and Walter Geichie
(1745-1837). Hill's horizontal compositions
follow those of Wilkie — for example, in *Pitlessie
Fair* 1804, (coll. National Galleries of Scotland)
— in the arrangement of groups of figures strung
out across the fore- and middle-ground of the
picture. This calotype, however, is even closer to
the work of Geichie, who made a number of
studies of the fisherfolk of the Firth of Forth
earlier in the century. Geichie's small
compositions, for example, *Three Fishwives*,
crayon 11.1 × 13.6 cm, and *Fishermen and
Fishwives*, pen and ink 11.4 × 16.8 cm (both
coll. National Galleries of Scotland), contain only
a few figures and have the same informal
atmosphere found in the Newhaven calotypes.
K.B.

109. Newhaven beach
SNPG, N62. Size 4
A view along the beach at Newhaven shows
fishing boats pulled up on the shingle. K.B.

110. Mrs. Flucker
SNPG, N10. Size 4. Reproduced p. 14
One of at least four variants (SNPG, N9, N11,
N12) shows Mrs. Flucker opening oysters as she
would on the streets of Edinburgh. In 1888 Mrs.
Cupples remarked: ''Times were long past,
when 'schoolboys would buy a dozen for a half-
penny at the luncheon hour, swallow them in
quick succession as they were opened, and then
partly close by giving the fishwife a kiss in
exchange for a thirteenth oyster.'' (Cupples,
Newhaven, its origin and history, Edinburgh, 1888,
p. 56) K.B.

111. Unknown group
SNPG, N58. Size 4
The loose arrangement of figures in this group
may also be found in the work of Scottish
painters such as David Wilkie, notably in his
painting, *Sir Walter Scott and His Family* 1817
(coll. SNPG). K.B.

**112. Mrs. Logan, Mrs. Seton and
two unknown men**
GUL 440. Size 4

**113. Mrs. Logan, Mrs. Seton and
two unknown men**
GUL 767, calotype negative for cat. 112. Size 4

**114. Alexander Rutherford,
William Ramsay and John Liston**
GUL 423. Size 4
This is one of the liveliest of Hill and Adamson's
portraits of Newhaven fishermen. Their relaxed
pose contrasts sharply with the sentimental
manner in which their dangerous occupation
was treated in some sections of the press. The
Ladies' Cabinet, for example, treated its readers
to poems addressed *To the Fisherman's
Daughter* (vol. 24, 1843, p. 437) and *The
Fisher's Wife* (vol. 23, 1843, p. 305). the latter
an appeal to the sea to bring her husband safely
home over the ''giant crests of foam''. K.B.

115. Unknown women
GUL 436. Size 4

116. Unknown women
GUL 430. Size 4

EDINBURGH

**119. Dugald Stewart Monument,
Calton Hill, Edinburgh**
GUL 406. Size 3
The monument was designed by William Henry
Playfair in the early nineteenth century.
The structure stood a short way above Hill
and Adamson's studio at Rock House on Calton
Hill. K.B.

**117. Greyfriars' Churchyard, the Naismith
Monument with Thomas Duncan and
D.O. Hill**
SNPG, E51. Size 4
Greyfriars' Churchyard in Edinburgh was the
setting for many Hill and Adamson calotypes, a
number of which were commissioned by George
Harvey for his painting *Children Blowing
Bubbles in Greyfriars' Churchyard* (*Paper and
Light* p. 134). As a report in *Chamber's
Edinburgh Journal* for 1836 makes clear the
cemetery was an important picturesque subject.
"The cemetery is now several acres in extent,
and besides the remains of countless multitudes
of ordinary people, contains the ashes of many
of the most distinguished men produced in
Scotland during the last three centuries. It may
indeed be called the metropolitan cemetery of
the country — the Westminster Abbey of
Scotland . . . Fashion having in some measure
deserted this quarter of the town . . . the place
has a decayed and venerable appearance . . .
while the scenery around — the stupendous
Castle . . . and the steeples and towers of the
. . . city — conspire still further to increase the
effect." (Vol IV, 1836, p. 109). K.B.

118. Greyfriars' Churchyard
GUL 412. Size 4

120. Mons Meg
Modern salt print by Michael Gray
GUL 462 (negative). Size 1
Mons Meg was a large cannon which was
mounted on the battlements of Edinburgh
Castle. Hill included it in his painting of
Edinburgh from the Castle (collection National
Galleries of Scotland). K.B.

121. High Tolbooth Church, Edinburgh
Calotype negative
GUL 476. Size 1

122. The Mound, Edinburgh
Calotype negative
GUL 464. Size 1. Reproduced p. 38

123. Greyfriars' Churchyard, Edinburgh
Calotype negative
GUL 453. Size 1

124. *View of Edinburgh from the Castle*
Modern salt print by Michael Gray
GUL 489 (negative). Size 1

The four prints (cats. 124, 125, 126, 127) comprise an overlapping panorama of Edinburgh as seen from the Castle. The photographs were taken from David's Tower directly above the semicircular ramparts of the Half Moon Battery.

Largely because of their size, the photographs provide a valuable record of the appearance of Edinburgh in the late 1840s. The Royal Scottish Academy and the Sir Walter Scott Monument are prominent in the middle ground of the left hand print. To the left of the Academy is the spire of St. Andrew and St. George, and the Lord Melville Monument (in St. Andrew Square) is visible between the Academy and the Scott Monument. The Monument to Frederick, Duke of York, (on the Esplanade) and the Ramsay Lodge occupy the foreground of the second photograph. Behind and in the center are the Waverley Bridge (under construction) and North Bridge (both bridges were rebuilt 1894-97). Calton Hill with the prominent Nelson Monument occupies the background with the Calton Jail and Governor's House (now largely incorporated into St. Andrew's House) below and to the right. The Spires of the Tolbooth Church and St. Giles are seen in the center of the third photograph. On the right hand side, St. Columba by the Castle is shown under construction. In the right hand photograph, Greyfriars' Church and Yard, the Charity Workhouse, and George Heriot's School (Hospital) occupy the background.

The negatives are undated. From the combined evidence of the construction progress and the payment records to the contractors for work on St. Columba by the Castle, a date in April, 1846, seems likely.[1]

There are no surviving contemporary prints. In light of this, the purpose may have been to provide study material for the background of Hill's painting, *Edinburgh Old and New*, now in the National Galleries of Scotland.[2] While there are strong similarities between the photographs and the painting, construction on St. Columba by the Castle and Waverley Bridge is shown completed in the painting, thereby suggesting a date before 1850 when construction began on the National Gallery of Scotland. Hill also used photographs of a group of the 42nd Gordon Highlanders, one of Newhaven fishwives, and John Ban Mackenzie (cat. 27), as studies for this painting.[3]

Panoramas of Edinburgh were by no means unusual, but the majority were made from Calton Hill and there are few precedents for Hill's choice of viewpoint.[4] What was novel in Hill's painting was the incorporation of both the old and new towns within one picture. The painting shows a prosperous city with the train terminal occupying an harmonious place in the center of the city. Michaelson has suggested that the painting was commissioned by John Miller (1805-83), the engineer of the Waverley Bridge and the owner of several of Hill's paintings with engineering subjects.[5] D.H.

1. Letter from Tristram Clarke, Scottish Record Office, to the author, 31 July 1986.
2. The painting has been identified with the succession of paintings of similar titles exhibited at the Royal Scottish Academy in 1848, 1863, and 1880 (See Michaelson, pp. 30 and 50). The painting is reproduced in Stevenson, *David Octavius Hill and Robert Adamson*, 24.
3. Stevenson, *David Octavius Hill and Robert Adamson*, pp. 26-27. The negatives of the 42nd Gordon Highlanders (in the collection of the Edinburgh Photographic Society) are dated April 9, 1846.
4. See *The Edinburgh Scene. Catalogue of Prints and Drawings in the Edinburgh Room, Central Public Library* (Edinburgh: Public Library Committee, 1951), 76-80.
5. Michaelson, pp. 10, 22-23, 30-31. The catalogues of the Royal Scottish Academy list Miller as the lender of a painting, *Old and New Edinburgh from the Castle*, for the years 1863 and 1880.

---

125. *View of Edinburgh from the Castle*
Modern salt print by Michael Gray
GUL 491 (negative). Size 1

---

126. *View of Edinburgh from the Castle*
Modern salt print by Michael Gray
GUL 493 (negative). Size 1. Reproduced p. 67

---

127. *View of Edinburgh from the Castle*
Modern salt print by Michael Gray
GUL 495 (negative). Size 1

LANDSCAPE

128. Fence and Trees in Colinton Wood
SNPG, L44. Size 4. Reproduced p. 37
This calotype has been attributed on stylistic
grounds to Adamson alone (by Richard R.
Brettell et al. in *Paper and Light. The Calotype
in France and Great Britain, 1839-1870,*
Boston, David R. Godine, 1984, p. 97). However,
the careful angling of the fence and the massing
of the two trees are similar to the small,
intimate drawings of artists such as Constable,
and, as such, are just as likely to have reflected
the sensibility of Hill, himself a landscape
painter and illustrator. K.B.

129. Ivy Covered Tree at Colinton
SNPG, L45. Size 4
In the British Library album of Hill and
Adamson's calotypes, this print is titled "The
Fairy Tree at Colinton." K.B.

130. Burnside, Fife
GUL LSP. Size 4
This calotype is unusually successful in view of
the chemically insensitive green of the foliage.
The print, in the collection of the Gernsheim
Collection, University of Texas, Austin, is signed
by Adamson, which has lead to suggestions that
the work was produced by him alone (see
Richard R. Brettell et al. in *Paper and Light.
The Calotype in France and Great Britain,
1839-1870,* Boston, David R. Godine, 1984,
p. 97). K.B.

131. Bonaly, Henning and Hill
GUL LSP. Size 4

Cat. 126 *View of Edinburgh from the Castle*